DAVOR GRÜN

INDUSTRIAL DESIGN

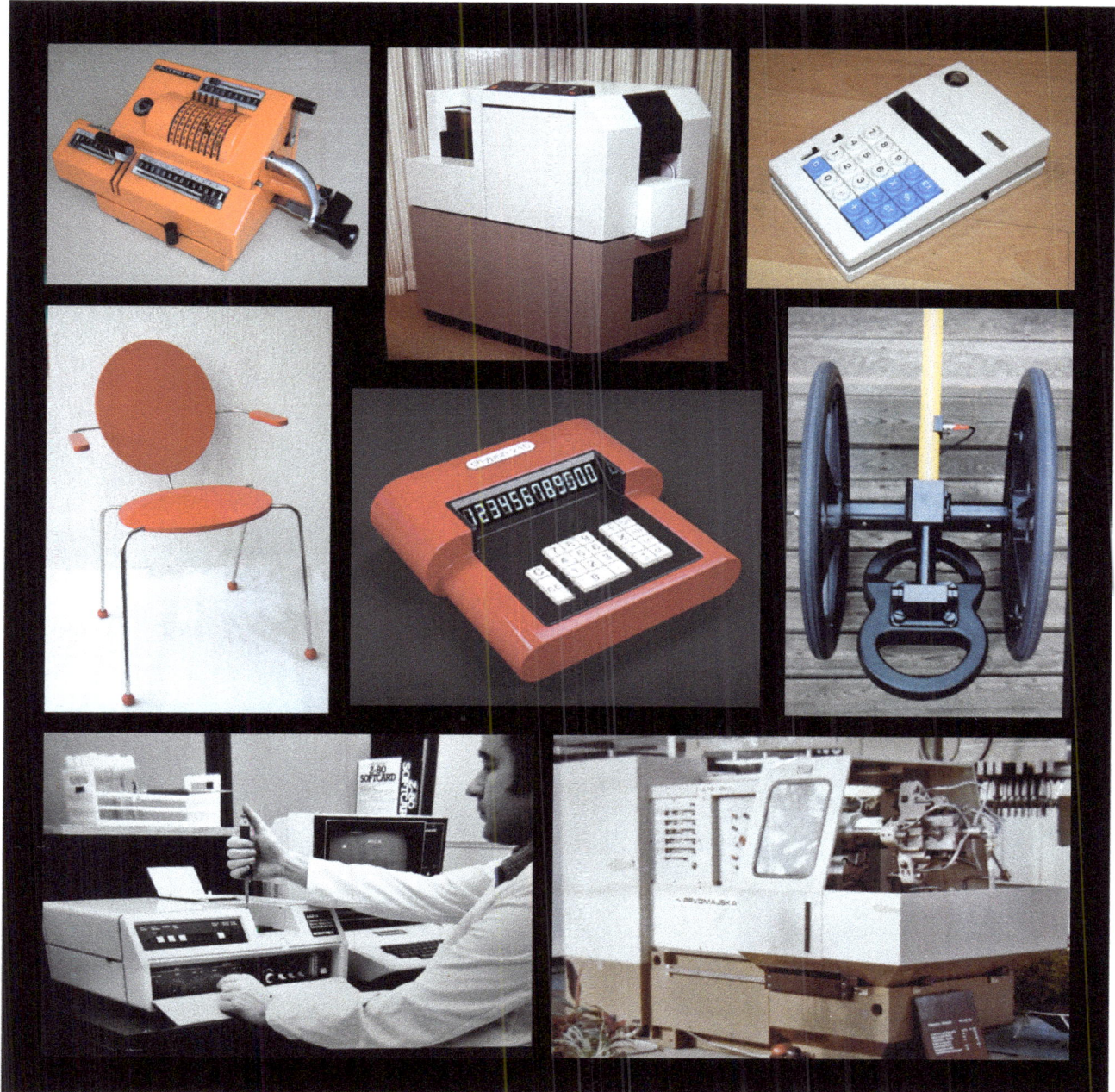

MONOGRAPH

Davor Grünwald

Industrial Design

Monograph

ISBN:

July, 2020

Toronto, Canada

Comments: dvgrunwald@hotmail.com

CONTENT

6 Instead of foreword

7 Introduction to life

8 Zagreb

8 Vienna story

10 Diploma

12 Zagreb story

14 The case of Croatian – Canadian industrial designer

15 Why did Davor Grünwald left?

19 Canadian story

23 Design of Products of Limited Production and Distribution

26 Why the Curtain of Silence Falls ?

31 In the last system, home savvy was treated as excess

40 Centuries of Croatian Design (clips)

42 Problem of the continuity – Davor Grünwald

43 Davor Grünwald – Retrorama of Industrial Design, 1968. -2008.

43 Danijel Maxsymiuk, speech by Canada's Ambassador

45 Pioneer of Design in Industry

49 The ULUPUH Lifetime Achievement Award, 2017.

49 Speech by Davor Grünwald – Lifetime Achievement Award

50 Sculptra, 1964.

51 Sculptra, first application, 2020

52 Sculptra, architectural module, 2020.

52 TRS – Factory of calculating machines

53 Trademark of the Factory of calculating machines 1970

53 Redesign of mechanical calculator, Calcorex, 1969.

54 Electronic table calculators (1970–1974)

54 TRS501, Electronic, table calculator, 1971.

55 TRS527, Battery calculator, 1973.

56 TRS533, Electronic, table calculator, 1974.

56 Pocket calculator, Minilog 37, 1969.

57 Chipon 210, Electronic calculator, 1971.

57 YU – DESIGN, 1972. – 1973.

59 Machine tool factory "Prvomajska"

59 Redesign of mass machine tools for Prvomajska

60 Metal furniture factory "Jadran"

61 Working chairs for operators, Jadran, 1972.

61 Electronic scale, TTM, 1973.

62 MICOM – PRODESIGN – VERSITAL

62 Computer Design Micom 2000, 1976

63 Pop – up booth, cooking utensils, Prodesign, 1977.
64 Versital tractor redesign, 1978.
64 Geophysical industry in Canada
64 SCINTREX
65 Atomic absorption spectrophotometer AAZ-2,
66 Transmitter and RECEIVER SE-88, Genie, 1982.
67 DELPHAX SYSTEMS
68 Corporate Identities of Delphax, 1983.
69 Fast ion printer – Delphax, 1981 – 1984.
72 GEONICS LTD
73 Conductivity Meter EM38, Geonics, 1985.
73 Encapsulated geophysical antenna, Geonics, 1986
74 EM39, Winch for geophysical probes, Geonics, 1990.
75 EM61–Geophysical instrument to find toxic waste
76 Protem geophysical instrument, 2001.
76 Land Mine finding device, Geonics, 2002.
77 SENSORS & SOFTWARE
78 Digital underground radar PulseEKKO 100, 1994.
79 GEM SYSTEMS
79 Geophysical Bird, Gem Systems, 2008.
80 CONCEPTS / UNREALIZED WORKS
80 Oxygen production machine, sketches, 1990
80 Disassembled wine/oil barrel, sketches, 2003.
81 Self-initiated works since 2008 to date
81 Rack for Porsche Boxster, 2011.
82 Chair Ellips, 2015.
83 Bike safety stick, 2016. Saves lifes!
84 Historically important trademarks design by D. G
85 Interesting questions with Jasna Lovrinčević
88 Davor Grünwald, a welcome speech at the exhibition at TMNT, 2019.
88 Exhibition at TMNT in Zagreb, 2019
92 Comments from the book of impressions TMNT
93 Industrial design tailored by man
100 Comments on my professional presentation
101 Conversation with Davr Grünwald for ORIS magazine
112 Biography of Davor Grünwald
114 Collected "thumbnails" from the life of Davor Grünwald
114 The Monster
115 Early Childhood
115 The fall
116 Drowning
117 The Runner
117 Yin & Yang
118 In the sand
119 JNA (Yugoslav army)

121 Silent Exercise
121 Almost tragedy
122 Summer downpour
122 Winter
123 House
123 Café
124 Children
124 Wife Vanja
125 Krk
125 Garage
126 Operations
126 Gabriel
128 What a character
128 Smart
128 Friend
129 Naked Island, prison
130 Famous Grünwalds'
130 Prof. Josip Grünwald
131 Prof. Mladen Grünwald
132 About Zeljko Borčić
133 No time
133 Accent
133 Lady Diana
134 What behaviour
134 Business drama
135 Floods
136 $ 100 000
137 AMCA
138 My NOW, since retiring in 2008. to date
139 Impressions of the state of industrial design in Croatia
140 2CV, Ugly duckling
143 Croatian Telecom
143 Everyday's dynamic
145 Email to the friend
145 Police station, Brač
146 Review of the review
146 List of the good ones
149 List of the bad ones
150 The final word

INSTEAD OF FOREWORD

I invited my colleagues, who know me in "soul," followed me and wrote articles in newspapers and magazines about me and my industrial design work, to write me a commemorative review for my Grant Monograph. I've been waiting for them, so it's been almost a year. Everyone promised to write something, but I didn't get anything from anyone (like it has been agreed among them!). I also sent those reminders, nothing! However, there is a great "common denominator": Corona virus and earthquake in Zagreb! These circumstances affect everyone negatively; it is a matter of surviving the crisis caused by these two events, it definitely reflects the time we live in at the moment. That's why I have a lot of understanding for that shut-up.

There, I explain to myself the "curtain of the silence", a colleagues who are otherwise represented in this Grand Monograph, all in one place for possible future analysis of history of Croatian/Canadian industrial design. To all who are shown in: "List of good once" - at the end of the book, I express my deepest gratitude.

Davor Grünwald

Davor Grünwald, 26

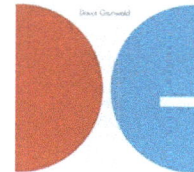

D. Grünwald emblem - B. Ljubičić design

Introduction to life

I was born during the Second World War, March 20. 1943. In Zagreb, Croatia. I was nine months old when my father lost his life 1944. in a train which was blown up by partisans expecting German officers. He was 32 years old and my mother 27. I was placed in the category: "The children of fascist's victims '. I past my school years without any problems. I was the athlete/runner and my speciality was 1000 and 1500 meters. I was dealing with radio amateurism – one and two bulbs radios. At the carpenter, "tišler" in the neighborhood, I was making housings for my electronic creations. Then, I did not know that I behave like a designer.

Grand Matura 1961. was very simplified. I just had to choose the subject and process it all in the small details. I decided to deal with physics, measurement device for voltage, resistance and amps. I made a wooden housing and painted it in red (this is when my "red phase" started which is still lasting). All professors and my fellow students were thrilled with my project. I did not know why I did it this way – I was simply following some of mine imbedded instincts.

After I completed gymnasium I went to Munich, Germany and was working as a technician in Siemens Halske for a year. From the savings I bought my mother a Grunding TV. At that time the people were watching TV in the shop windows. I returned to Zagreb and enrolled in Electronic faculty. In the second semester my life was heading in different directions......

Zagreb, Croatia
I was born and I will be buried there

Vienna story 1964. – 1968.

..... In spring 1964. in Museum of Arts and Crafts (MUO) in Zagreb it was presented the exhibit of Italian design. After I have been trough the exhibit, I become stunned and told myself: **This is me!** I have to become the designer, but how and where? I decided to explore this secretly and find out the answers. I did not want to create an alarm. Soon I discovered at the corner of the building " Center for Industrial Design" established a year ago. The head of the Center was Zvonimir Radić, "Diša", professor at the Academy of Art. He knew all about

Industrial Design and he recommended me to visit the only I D School in Europe, in Ulm, Germany. He also mentioned that there is something at Academy of Applied Design in Vienna. I decided to check these schools out. I could not get the tourist visa for Germany, but I got the Austrian. So I went to Vienna on my scooter Vespa. Professor Hoffman, the head of the Industrial Design department, explained to me that the entrance exam will be in the autumn and he advised me how to prepare myself for that. I notified my mother about my decision and that I will stay in Vienna. Of course, this was shocking news for her! I found the accommodation in "Jugend Herberge" hostel for young people. When my visa expired a policeman picked me up and brought me at the police station. They explained to me that they will send me by train back to Yugoslavia. One higher, ranging policeman whispered in my ear that if someone of great reputation in Austria would sign the guaranty letter for me, I could stay. I remembered that my aunt gave me a name of her friend in case I need the help. This gentleman signed the letter without any questions. Unfortunately, several years later I read in the newsletter that he lost his life during some kinds of political demonstrations. He was named, the firs political victim after the war.

I found the accommodation in the family of Croatian decent in Schwechat, the suburb of Vienna where the Vienna airport is located. I was working in their garden and whatever they needed in exchange for accommodation. I was cruising on my Vespa around the Burgenland and sketched the villages. I also made a few practical items. I made some money as a statist and thicket controller in Vienna opera.

For the entrance exam at the Academy 30 candidates came. The tests lasted three days and they were demanding. I was one of the five accepted. Already in the second semester I had justified prof. Hoffman's confidence on me. He gave us an assignment; to create an element which, if multifold, could be connected vertically and could not be disassembled horizontally. I was a good mathematician and felt that a solution could be found in the trigonometric functions sign and cosign. That year, the word congress of industrial design (ICSID) was held in Vienna. My element (module) was shown in the exhibit and created a small sensation among the participants. This module, later on, I named SCULPTRA and protected design and the name. And today, 54 years later, my wife and I are entertaining us with searching for applications for this shape. It becomes my three-dimensional emblem of my Industrial Design approaches. 1965. Museum of Art and Craft in Zagreb was presented the exhibit by the name: New Tendencies 3. I participated with my ten Sculptra, 12 x 12 cm, in different colours. After the exhibit was closed, I came to pick my modules, but I was told it was stolen!

Professor Hoffmann was given us often small assignments, designing of products for local factories. It was like a competition among our students. I often won which was not welcomed by my fellow students. One such product was: "Machine for anthropological measurements for ergonomic application". That was before the computers and lasers. That is, where my fascination with ergonomic was established.

In order to survive I had to work at odd jobs, whatever I could get. Once I was hired by Mr. Urban, the owner of the factory which was making products based on the food for the bees Queen. I got the "Mini", small car to deliver the products to pharmacies in Vienna and surrounding. In exchange I got the apartment to live, in the second district, "Becirk". The factory owner and his family lived in a villa in the elite part of the city, "Grincing". Every Sunday I was having lunch with them. One day Mr. Urban invited me for a meeting. He explained to me that his son, astrologer, indicated to him that the stars are telling him that I have excellent character. He offered me the leading position in his factory and I am welcome to marry his daughter – she was a good friend of mine. The only condition was I have to give up my industrial design study. I declined! In the last year of my study I received the scholarship from Austrian government for good foreign students. Now I could concentrate on my diploma assignment: Microchip station, this was the technology of that time to archive the data in Bibliotheca. Unfortunately, I have no photos of that.

Diploma, 1968.

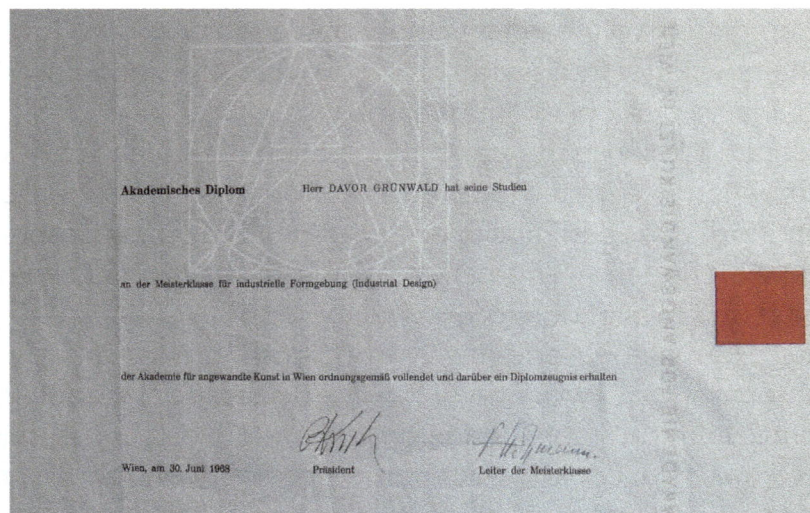

"The linking of very good general with technical knowledge, assiduousness and diligence, talents for invention, and creative ability with excellent qualities of character qualify Mr. Grünwald in the best manner to be an Industrial Designer."

Franz Hoffman, Professor Arch.

Akademie fur Angewandte Kunst   Vienna, 1968.

Davor Grünwald (1943.) got his diploma from the Academy of Applied Arts in Vienna, department Industrial Design 1968. He then spends nine months at the specialization on Institute for Industrial Design, working on tool machine ergonomic. This way he becomes first formally educated Industrial Designer in Croatia (Yugoslavia). He returned to Zagreb where he together with V. Žitković and A. Karavanić has established department of Industrial Design at ULUPUH (Association of Artists and Applied Artists in Croatia). He also initiated the YU-DESIGN, Industrial Design Award, which was active 1972. and 1973. at Zagreb fair.

**STUDIO ZA
INDUSTRIJSKI
DIZAJN**

Prodesign emblem

PRODESIGN   **"On behalf of design"**
PRO   **From Latin: "for, on behalf of"**
DESIGN   **From Latin: Designare, "to designate"**
Modern meaning of DESIGN: As intentional creation of a plan of construction of an object.

Most likely that the compound PRODESIGN was used the first time in the world **1968.** when my consulting office was established after I received my diploma at Academy for Applied Arts in Vienna.

*

When he arrived in Zagreb he has established a Design Studio Prodesign. As a freelance designer he designed numerous electronic calculators for Factory of Calculating Machines (TRS, 1969. – 1974.), machines tools for Prvomajska (1969. -1974.), and the chairs next to the machines for factory workers, with the help of "Jadran", factory of metal furniture (1973.).

For the redesign of machine tools for Prvomajska , 1974., he received, then the youngest recipient, the city of Zagreb Award and later golden plaque in Leipzig, Germany.
Very soon after that 1975. since all his contracts with his clients were cancelled by the Government of Yugoslavia, he left Croatia for Canada, first Montreal and Winnipeg , and than 1980. in Toronto. In Montreal, short time, he works for Micom (1976.) and Prodesign (1977.) (the same name as his studio in Zagreb). In 1980. He started his consulting company by the name Inventive Products Design (IPD). He got hired by Scintrex in Toronto, but after one year he left them and joined Delphax Corporation (1981. 1986.). For them, he designed fast ion deposition printers, corporate identity and exhibition system. In1985. he was employed by Geonics, geophysical company until his retirement 2008. All these years he acted as consultant for Sensors & Software and Gem Systems, all geophysical companies. Therefore, he practically had a monopoly as industrial designer in the Canadian geophysical industry. During his Canadian activity he designed tractors, computers, geophysical systems, geophysical "birds" and other highly sophisticated technological devices. After he retired, he continued with design work, but now without industrial background. From the beginning of his carrier, he was a member of professional Associations in Croatia and Canada. From 1990. – 2000. he was the vice president of AMCA (Association of ex students of Croatian Universities). He is an emeritus member of ULUPUH and HDD (Croatian Design Association).
Marko Golub and Koraljka Vlajo

Austria, Burgenland, 1967. D. Grünwald

Zagreb story, 1968. – 1975.

I returned to Zagreb with great anticipation. CIO's head was now Mario Antonini, the absolvent of the Academy of Applied Arts which was moved to Belgrade. The architects, who were designing the furniture, like; Bernardi. Richter, Petranović , ... design theoretic; Mestrovć, Kritovac, Keller...they all gathered in CIO. Antonini's agenda was to get me as well, but I did not like the idea to have a mentor. With the help of Žitkovć and Karavanić I initiated Department of Industrial Design within the ULUPUH (Croatian Association of Applied Arts). Through ULUPUH I got the freelance status and the social insurance. I started mu consulting business PRODESIGN, designed my trade mark and printed my stationary.
One morning came two policemen's to my mother's apartment, in which was my studio. They accused me that I have illegal company and they confiscated all materials. They also told me, if I open up illegal studio again, they will put me in jail. Private enterprise was not allowed in communist Yugoslavia. Despite all this I was ready to pay a visit to all factories in Zagreb and surroundings.

Unfortunately, Yugoslav army came along to get me! They send me to Strumica, diagonally across Yugoslavia in Macedonia, the garrison for "suspicions' " My captain told me that I have to stay in the army for two years since the army does not recognize the foreign Universities (what a nonsense!). Academy for Applied Arts in Belgrade had nostrified my diploma. After one year I returned to Zagreb and I continued where I stopped a year ago.

Wherever I went I ran into CIO "traces". Most likely they were expensive and acted monopolistic. Relatively easy I got contracts with factory directors like; Factory of calculating machines, Prvomajska - machine tools, the scale factory and others. The cooperation went smoothly with all and the results followed. I received the city of Zagreb Award for tool machine designs 1973. I was the youngest recipients (30). It was given to me by the famous City of Zagreb major Večeslav Holjevac. The Award I shared with architect Marijan Haberle, the architect of Vatroslav Lisinski concert hall.

Category for Industrial Design did not exist so the organizers solved the problem; they gave to Mr. Haberle the golden plaque and I received a substantial amount of Dinars. It looked like I was born under happy star.

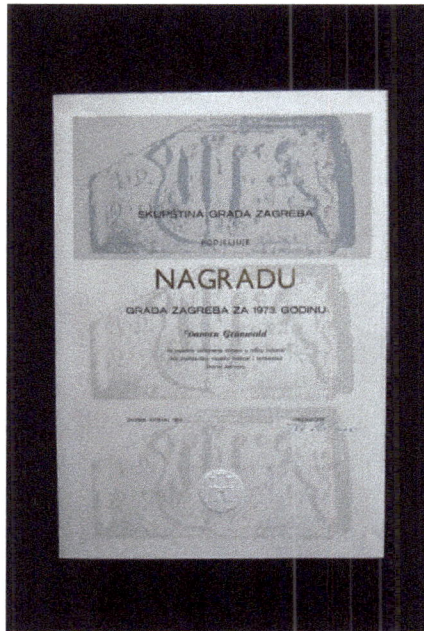

City of Zagreb Award, 1973.

Davor Grünwald, 30

While I was working on tool machines I noticed that the machine operators were sitting on boxes. I designed chairs for this application. The director of Jadran, metal furniture factory, invited me for a discussion. One day before, I met my four years younger colleagues, Marijan Oresić, who recently received the same diploma for Industrial Design in Vienna. I told him the happy news about the meeting with Jadran. When I came at a meeting that Monday at 2 PM the director asked me who Marijan Oresić was? I explained that he is my friend and I am his best man at his wedding. The director told me that Marijan came that day in 6 AM and offered himself for this position, Director of Design and Research, which was intended for me. I got this well paid job! Three months later director invited me for discussion, he told me that since I am now in leading position I have to join the Communist party. My answer was: "No thank you". I turned around and left Jadran for good. Before that I managed to assure the scholarship for Marijan's younger brother Mladen, who also studied in Vienna. Later on them both ended up as professors at the Design Studio in Zagreb (Within Architect Faculty).
I continued successfully in a freelance capacity. My euphoria did not last for long. Yugoslav government came up with the decision that the state factories are not permitted to use the services of private persons. Even today I am under the impression that this nonsense was initiated by Antonini (grand Communist). I am also under the impression that he is the one who informed the police that I have illegal studio. All my contracts become void "over the night" and I was forced to look for the solutions abroad. Finally I decided to immigrate to Canada.

The case of Croatian – Canadian industrial designer Davor Grünwald

is exceptionally intriguing for various reasons. The word is about the author who within six years of intensive activity in Croatia and Yugoslavia left his mark on local industrial design history, and who after that continued for several decades, with the same intensity, activity in Canada. He is a designer whose professional traces, very picturesque, presents the surrounding condition for design, his specific social/economic context, as well as the circumstances which dictated the position of the designer and his role. Already during the first dialogue, conducted before preparation for this exhibition and publication, the way Davor Grünwald speaks about his profession, it impressed us his avid credential in his mission, his integrity and principled under any cost. Grunwalds' biography is impressive and exciting, mostly owing to his determined, forceful and strong character. If we follow how he got his design assignments by the end of the sixties; TRS, Prvomajska, Jadran and others, than very strong economic actors and today the post-transition industrial ruins, the most of these stories start with requesting to talk to directors. His self confident approach would end up with the same tone if he would detect that the particular arrangement is harmful for his integrity and status. On the other hand, if we observe the span of his designs from the late sixties until the retiring 2008. and later, it is evident that non of design assignments is less important, and that there is no context specifically exclusive so it does not deserves integral, through thought design treatment.

Besides his famous electronic calculators for Factory of calculating machines (TRS) and fast printers for Delphax company at mid eighties and the few exceptions (computer Micom 2000) the most realized products, Grünwald has designed, are not consumer products but belong to scientific industrial field. These are; massive machine tools for Prvomajska, ergonomic chairs for Jadran, geophysics equipment for Geonics, Sensors & Software, Gem Systems, which are used specifically by geophysical scientists. Grünwald is, like all other designers, very aware of the prestige which his work is created, working for strong industries, keeping certain autonomy since most of the time he was working as a freelance. Finally, he commented it was not his conscience decision that his professional opus is based on the relation between man and machine (the way Bernardo Bernardi formulated for Zagreb Design Award – machines tools for Prvomajska). And for sure, all what he realized in Croatia and Canada there is a common denominator, the man united with technology, the one who operates with heavy machinery or equipment for scanning the soil, all the time in interaction and mutually fulfilment.

Marko Golub and Koraljka Vlajo

*

I had several interesting interviews beginning of seventies last centuries until now, the beginning of 21 centuries. In all of them there is "common denominator" constant negative social/economic background in industrial design in Croatia.
I feel that it is my obligation to publish all these interviews in my Grand Monograph.

Goroslav Keller, 1975. " Maybe this Croatian economy is not ready jet to accept such access to design. Personnel wise, technology wise, organizing wise, not ready jet. We will assume that the time did not come for the application of design methodology, which Davor Grünwald has offered.... "

.... and 2020. (45 years later!) Sonja Lebos wrights ...." in this post-industrial time, in the country which the industry has been totally ruined, so even industrial design does not have much sense"

Goroslav Keller, 1975,

Why Davor Grünwald left?
About the departure to Canada of recipient of City of Zagreb Award for design

While you are reading these lines, Davor Grünwald will already flu over the ocean, trying in faraway Canada to secure the existence for his wife, seven year old daughter and himself in sharp professional competition. But why are we noticing that? Because the case of Davor Grünwald is partially characteristic of the condition in our design.

Davor Grünwald is industrial designer. He is one of the few professionals in our society. The man who considered design as his profession and hobby. The man who – after he returned from Vienna, where he studied design – was very soon noticed in our domestic professional field, after all, after very serious approach toward the design solution of industrially produced objects. The man who approached his assignments by intuition, rationally, scientifically and emotionally...

He was born 1943. in Zagreb. He completed his gymnasium education in Zagreb and after that studied electronics for two years, which influenced his design approaches – exact scientifically, rational methods, besides electronics remained his passion as well.

At "Academy for Applied Arts" in Vienna, he studied at the industrial design department and got his diploma 1968. After that, he spent nine months at the Industrial Design Institute studding tool machines ergonomics.

As a finished designer, all around professional who "baked his trade" (if we could talk about design as a trade), Grünwald got involved immediately in professional life. Trough professional Association of Applied Artists of Croatia (ULUPUH), he was initiator and the founder of the industrial design department at ULUPUH, and initiator and the member of the action comity of jugging of industrial design at Zagreb fare – YU-DESIGN. Furthermore, he was a member of education comity and Art council of ULUPUH. As indicated, he was socially extremely committed, but at the same time he was preaching that design has to be proven through practice, professional work. In several Zagreb factories (just to mention few: Factory of calculating machines (TRS), Factory of machine tools Prvomajska, Factory of scales and others) Grünwald found business partners with which he accomplished successful and fruitful cooperation.

Redesign of mechanical & design of several electr. calculators, pocket calc. electr. scale,1969-1975.

The winner of City of Zagreb Award, 1973.

In "Jadran", where he was, for a short time, employed as director of R & D, Grünwald realized some furniture's. But he is more intriguing with design problems which are on the border of design affinity. Despite all they are very important and therefore need a designer's intervention. These are for examples chairs for workshops, for industry, and medical chairs of special applications. These are the products which require strict design – valorisation, projects which could be realised by applying truly design synthesis of various interdisciplinary conditions and requests.

Automatic lathe

Automatic sharpener

For design of a series of machine tools for Prvomajska, Grünwald received **"City of Zagreb Award" 1973.** (The youngest recipient, 30). The same series received a golden plaque at world fair in Leipzig. It is about the family of automatic lathes AT-250, tool sharpeners Geometric 430. In explanation of City of Zagreb Award, Bernardo Bernardi explains: Despite the facts that he received his diploma 6 years ago and with this title of industrial designer from the Academy of Applied Arts in Vienna, Davor Grünwald has already, from his professional activity, numerous products which are circulating within the channels of trade distribution. In our industry the industrial design of heavy tool machines has no tradition,

Davor Grünwald took upon himself to resolve the most complex, and with product material value, very responsible problematic of industrial design. Designing machine tools for Prvomajska in Zagreb he approached the task with the only correct way – by analyzing all sensitive conditions which came from the relation between men – machine. He showed that he is capable the elements of ergonomics analyze; technical and technological conditions sensibiliser and unite complex requirement of high operational functionality. But his intervention   does not stop at the border of technical. His extraordinary sensibility for an art phenomenon he managed all rational instrumentation and required technical facts "translate" into visual reality and harmonic art unity. This way these machines become important elements of the overall atmosphere of working environment.

. Redesign of machines tools for Prvomajska, models 1:10, 1970.1074.

Among others, here is Factory of Calculating Machines (TRS). In cooperating with this factory, which found in Grünwald not only business partner and expert, but almost house designer. Grünwald found possibility to integrate all his professional interest. His knowledge of electronics from one side and ergonomics, production technologies, and knowledge of modern materials on the other side, it came to a full expression.

Redesign of mechanic calculator CALCOREX 403 was his first assignment after he returned from Vienna. Therefore, acquaintance between designer and corporation has already remarkable tradition. Trough this acquaintance Davor, before all, has good opportunity to get familiar with client's production technologies and possibilities of his client, and the client acquires larger trust to a young designer. This "bridge" of trust resulted in series of electronic calculators, just to mention some: TRS527, TRS501, and TRS533. For design of these calculators he received BIO Awards (Biennale of Industrial Design1973.), together for development of judging criteria YU-DESIGN (1973.) He received the SKOJ Award in the same year.

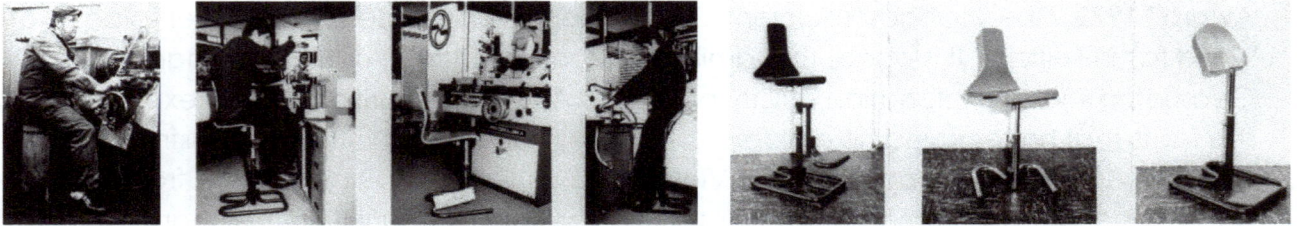

Industrial chairs for "Jadran", 1970. – 1972.

"I don't want to work less"

While we are sitting in his garsonere, adapted basement in the fact, I am impressed with attractiveness of all details of this residence. I do not have to wander of exceptional functionality of furniture elements. The lamp made of plastic oil canister and the cooling tube from "Fića", ashtray made of Sculptra – well, we are in the residents of designers. Namely, his wife Vanja is designer as well, specialized in interior products.

Playing with plastic sinusoid profiles, Davor explained to me that this theoretical assignment was the object of his study in Vienna. I never tried to find practical application for it. I was simply impressed by its geometrical characteristics and aesthetics.

Davor's standpoint regarding design is clearly defined by prof. Hoffmann's quote: One industrial object is being generated by planning and coordinating of factors from many structural levels and their organisations and not adding up various elements"

The discussion about Jadran situation: "I could stay in Jadran by accepting communist membership, and live worry free. Unfortunately, I think that being the alternatives, live worry free and not to work much, or try to do something and not live so worry free. I chose the second option. Because, one has to earn for living, He or she has to earn by working something useful, having the feeling that He or She earned that through honest work."

The Grünwald couple have not regular jobs; they are the ones of the few designers. Hitting the doors of domestic factories and offering their professional expertise, offering instead larpularistic bluffs and aesthetic platitudes, serious interdisciplinary approach – at the same time they understood uncertain existence of such work.

We don't want to attack our economy, our proverbial misunderstandings and not being aware of innovations, patents, designs and all progressive professional attitudes. Maybe this domestic economy is not, speaking objectively, Is not ready to accept such access to design. Personalize, technology, organization not ready, does not matter. We will assume that the time did not arrive yet to apply such design methodology and such access to design problems which Davor Grünwald has offered to us. We wish him happy journey, but still we would like him to come soon back, if design is what we are claiming, we will certainly need him.

Goroslav Keller, Why Davor Grünwald left? 1975. Creative communication

1975. He left Croatia for Canada, first in Toronto, then he moved to family member in Montreal, because of language barrier and financial difficulties. In Montreal, he will stay until 1978. Then he moved to Winnipeg because of political troubles in Quebec. Two years later he permanently settled down in Toronto.

Canadian story 1975 – now

I had well situated family member in Montreal and he invited me to come to Canada and stay with him. He would come for summer vacation to Istria. Part of my Grunwald family from Munich were nudists and they were coming to Premantura where a famous nudist camp is located. Nikica Turkovic was with them. And so one day I descent with my briefcase, naked and join them. Here you go what an industrial designer was forced to do for survival. That's when the deal fell in to travel to Canada. Nikica Turković had a window and door factory and promised to send me a guarantee letter. With that letter, I went to Belgrade to the Canadian Embassy, and after a year of waiting I got the documents. First I started working for Nikica Turković, he had an office building and a factory, and he was wealthy. He lived in a wealthy, English part of Montreal. I worked for him in exchange for housing. He also had one street with about 20 houses with four apartments and I kept them; painted apartments, mowed the lawn..... And then through the papers I started looking for a job in my profession. The paper was full of ads for designers. But they were "designers" for plumbing and the like. It was hard to discern, I wanted to work for a company that needed a "real" designer.

The first four years in Toronto, Montreal and Winnipeg went on to gather the so-called "Canadian experience," but my Canadian career really began in Toronto. "Do I have Canadian experience?"" I was asked frequently by potential employers. Well, I just got here! Since I didn't understand and spoke English very well, I couldn't get a better job. I went to Montreal when the relative called me to join him. I worked for two years in a metal furniture factory in electronics. The company closed when the owner died abruptly and I found myself on the labor market. It was a pretty dramatic experience for me. In the paper, I found an ad that "Texas Instruments" in the U.S. is looking for an industrial designer, educated in Europe with experience designing electronic calculators. The description fit my profile completely. I was invited to a three-day interview in Dallas. I even got a real estate agent. On the third day, they asked me where I was really from. My answer was, "From Yugoslavia!" The man changed his facial expression and said, "We can't see you, prepare for your return." I understood everything. Texas Instruments is a very strong U.S. military company. It is understood that they feared potential communist spies so they "blew on cold," and at that time the "Cold War" was on the world stage.

The wife, meanwhile, arrived with our daughter in Montreal. In 1977, our son was born. At the time, the activities of secession from Canada began in Quebec, and the Canadian French were very unpleasant towards the new emigrants. We had to leave Montreal. I had a very interesting situation in Winnipeg. Here I helped an American industrial designer, John Vanderhof, who had a well established consulting office. When he won the contract with the tractor factory Versital, we agreed that each of us would develop our own tractor concept.

Another young industrial designer participated in this. On the day of the presentation we had three concepts. The CEO of the tractor factory has carefully analyzed each solution. In the end, he pointed his hand at my drawings and said, "We will develop this further because it has a "European look" and that interests us." My boss wasn't happy, but he had to comply with the company president's decision.

The boss would sometimes go crazy in the uniform of green berets, which he preserved from the Vietnam War era. I had to leave him, and in return he tried to get back at me. Because of the brochure in which I presented my tractor concept, the boss reported me to Versital because, according to the lawyer, I published their trade secret. I was told I had to pay all the costs of developing the design. They invited me to talk. I spent three days in that beautiful city. I spoke to five professors and presented my projects. In the end, the dean told me that I was their first choice and that he would inform me in writing about the details. The letter arrived a month later. Within a year, I had to lose my accent to be accepted. I replied that I had noticed that all the people I spoke to had an accent - and that I would probably never lose mine. The professor's place, of course, I didn't get.

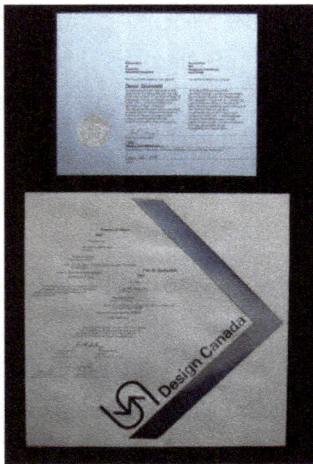

Design Canada Award, 1982.   Davor I Vanja Grünwald, son Mladen. 1982.

In Toronto, I got a job as a draftsman through an intermediary agency, so-called headhunters. I decided to join this geophysical company Scintrex through "small doors" and show through my work who I am. It took a year for the president to see that I was actually "something else." It was only after winning the Canadian Design Canada Award for geophysical device Genie, which was ergonomically demanding, that he invited me to talk. I gave him a lecture on industrial design and the role of industrial designer in the corporation. In the end, I asked him if he'd put me in that position and improve my salary. He turned me down smoothly! A week later, I found an ad for an industrial designer position at Delphax, founded by a runaway group of IBM. They were developing fast computer printers based on newly patented Ion deposition technology. It was a superior method than Xerox's laser method. The company had 51 percent Canadian and 49 percent U.S. capital. I got that job and twice my salary. I remember what pleasure I had I went to the president of a geophysical company and announce that I would leave the same day. Despite everything, I was their consultant for several years and charged high fees. The president admitted to me that he made a mistake.

That year, in 1980, I founded a consulting company and protected the name INVENTIVE PRODUCT DESIGN, briefly IPD. I used that for "side jobs" and tax write-offs.

In a new job, at a fast-printer company, things weren't going well. My boss was a mechanical engineer and he gave me engineering assignments. He did not realize that my function was to direct a group of engineers, who developed printing machines, towards the final product (ergonomics, functionality, aesthetics, choice of materials). He gave me poor performance assessments (the employee evaluation system). I had to do something drastic! For several months, I worked secretly at home on a fast printer concept designed to print reports quickly after conferences. In my garage, I made a non-functional, life-size model. I developed an entirely new corporate visual identity, including trademark application on products and printed material (that's what the president asked me to do because the Japanese delegation couldn't read the company's name). One Sunday, I put it all in the company president's room. That Monday, when I got to work early, I sat in my office waiting. Suddenly I heard a scream in the hallway of the company "Holly cow, who did this?" It was the president of the company. I came up to him and explained to him why I did it. He immediately informed his managers that I would directly answer to him and develop, in my own way, new concepts of applications. I got everything I asked for, a modelling shop, so I could express myself creatively, and I directed a team of engineers at the time. It was my most creative period in Canada. There was another incident when one of the company's managers ordered the design of a fast printer from an outside consulting firm owned by his friend. I was ordered to cooperate with this outside consultant. I refused and gave a lesson to this arrogant guy about decency and appropriate behavior within the corporation and suggested that I work in parallel on my version. Now the company could compare and choose between two concepts. They decided to produce my version.
The company, meanwhile, announced relocation of the headquarter office to Boston, the U.S. financial center. There was talk that the company would be taken over by Xerox. In the end, Xerox was able to destroy a potential competitor and they proceeded with its laser method. It was a typical method of action by strong American companies. About a dozen of us got an offer to move to Boston. I accepted, but I didn't want to go neck-and-neck and move the family. They agreed to pay for a return plane ticket once a month to Toronto and rent a car, The troubles arose three months later when the company decided to give a development contract to a Japanese company, including industrial design. I've become a technological surplus. That's when the provocations of my American boss, the vice president, began. He invited us all to the meeting and the first item on the agenda was a question directed to me. "Why did you design the new trademark in red? Didn't you know blue was a traditional American color?" Instead of explaining to them the real visual-graphic reasons, I replied: "Mr. Mastedino, have you forgotten that the company is still Canadian, and the traditional Canadian color is red! Look at the Canadian flag!" The man faded, then turned red (he didn't turn blue) and took a step out of the room. It was clear to me that he was trying to provoke me and impose, since I came from Yugoslavia, that I am promoting communist red colour on American soil. I was aware that with my response I defended

Canadian colors and the flag. That way I lost my well-paid job, but I was never sorry for doing that. The next morning, he pointed his hand towards the exit. I was told to pack in an hour time and I report to the Toronto Staff Management. The clerk in Toronto greeted me and said that I had given a verbal resignation in Boston and that I had to pay back all their money ($10-20,000!). I told her it was a lie and that the boss kicked me out and that under the contract I didn't owe them anything. I announced to her that I would sue the company for a wrongful dismissal. If I do that, she told me, I wouldn't be able to get a job in Canada anymore. The last thing I said to her was, "Watch me!"
I was told if that dispute had been resolved in America, I wouldn't have had a chance to get anything. I hired the best labor law lawyer in Canada. The trial lasted two years, and I won the dispute, as well as a large amount of damages. My former boss Mastedino was expelled from the company. I found out later that he was a CIA officer! After that experience, I realized that I wasn't interested in American arrogance and that I had to concentrate on Canada. With the money I fixed the house and lived for two years without income. The clerk defamed me in the worst possible way with potential employers and therefore for two years I couldn't get a job.

In the end, I managed to get a job at the geophysical company Geonics, where the vice president (later president/owner) was a colleague of mine, an athlete from Mladost at Sava in Zagreb. I spent 24 years with them until my retirement in 2008. Their electronic geophysical devices were already well received all over the world. They were protected with numerous electronic patents. However, ergonomics, functionality and aesthetics (shape elements) were simply not present. To my credit, these devices were treated with elements of industrial design, and today they are considered a good design. For the last few years, the vice president of the company, with whom I've had problems all those years, has been calling me derogatory names in front of employees, old shithead and old farts. I briefed the president on that, but he didn't do anything. I was ready to file a lawsuit for harassment. The president fired me and offered $100,000 in severance pay, provided I didn't sue them. I've accepted! During my 24 years working with Geonics, I had a consulting relationship with two other geophysical companies, Sensors & Software and Gem Systems. I became a specialist, industrial designer for geophysical devices, which can also be seen in the photographic map. Toronto is the world center of these technologies and I have participated in all of them: electromagnetic – Scintrex, Geonics, radar – Sensor & Software and which use earth magnetic field – Gem Systems. My solutions with strong ergonomic, functional and aesthetic elements are present in all these devices. In other words, I raised the quality of products in this otherwise neglected industry that did not know industrial design. Interestingly, the Croats own the strongest two geophysical companies in Canada.

I published an article in 1995. in ICSIDnews 4/95 magazine entitled: "Design of limited production and the product's distribution. In it, I argue that ICSID (ICSID) (International Council of Societies of Industrial Design) the definition of industrial design neglects 70% of the world's small-batch products. This definition mentions that only massively produced products are treated with elements of industrial design. I was the first, in 1995, to see this colossal error and injustice and insisted that two different product groups, mass and limited production should be mentioned in the ICSID ID definition. It wasn't until 2015, when ICSID changed its name to WDO (World Design Organization) in the ID definition, no group was mentioned, which is also not correct.

Design of Products of Limited Production and Distribution

By
Davor Grunwald

Davor
Grunwald,
MA. Dipl.
Industrial Design,
past Director
of ACID

The design of mass-produced electronic calculators was one of the first challenges I was to face as newly-trained in the field of industrial design.

Design challenge. Some 15 years later, when approached by a small company from Toronto, Canada to save one of their products from dying, one of the first questions I asked was: "What is your yearly production?" "Twenty units at most," was the answer! Though sceptical about the company, my curiosity finally prevailed and I took on the job.

This company became a world leader in electromagnetic technology applied in geophysical and environmental studies. The instruments and equipment they design are in the focal point of today's environmental issues, such as:
- ground water contamination detection in most industrialized countries in the world,
- ground water exploration, especially in such regions as sub-Saharan Africa,
- detection of buried toxic waste and
- soil salinity determination in mass crop production on farms.

Modern ideology. In this particular industry, a series of 50 units a year is a large number, and yet, all the aspects of the industrial design process are well represented. The products that have emerged have a "European" look. An entire authentically-Canadian industry was transformed into modern industrial design ideology.

To achieve this, experience with mass-produced products was required, as well as the ability to apply the same balancing act of the design process elements, which are very well defined in ICSID's industrial design definition. Of course, some materials and production technologies have been substituted with others which do not require large initial investment.

It is a proven fact that approximately 70% of the economical growth and employment by developed nations comes from small industries. By pushing the Industrial-Design-Ideology in this direction in an organized manner as well, a broad base of opportunities would be created for young industrial designers. At the same time, our social commitment to enhance the quality of life would be broadened.

Proposals. Based on this background, I recently submitted some proposals to ICSID. The first one entails adding the word "limited" twice to ICSID's Industrial Design definition:

"...The design process represents the method of creative thinking employed for the purpose of achieving through analysis, a three dimensional form intended for mass OR LIMITED production and mass OR LIMITED distribution. As the product is the result..."

My second proposal has to do with ICSID's endorsement practice. Companies and Societies pay a minimum $1,000 endorsement fee for industrial design-related activities. Recently, we witnessed the rebirth of nations out of ruins of a dark period of totalitarian political systems, now struggling to define their freedom. Our characteristic professional sensitivity should prevail and enable us to give at least our moral support to all design-related activities. Therefore, why not add a new category of endorsement with pure moralistic ideological dimensions, by simply waiving the endorsement fee?

To define their freedom, the mentioned nations have to re-activate a broad economical base: small industries' small series products. This is where a proposed change of ICSID's industrial design definition, and a new moralistic endorsement category definitely have a common ground. With the help of ICSIDnews, I am sure that many ICSID members would identify themselves as well with these views regarding the industrial design of products of limited production and distribution. **DG**

Digital ground penetrating radar

In Memoriam

On June 5, 1995, Wolfgang Swoboda, former ICSID Board Member and Director of Österreichisches Institut für Formgebung, died surrounded by his family and closest friends.

We sadly mourn the decease of Wolfgang Swoboda. He was known throughout the world of design for his extensive and innovative contributions.

As designers, we grew to appreciate and have respect for Wolfgang as a prominent personality in modern cultural life. He had an innate ability to take up a constructive and reassuring attitude toward the work and activities of his immediate circles. This happened even when he was already suffering from his illness. In the manner of a dear friend, his charming wife Uschi stood by him all the way.

Wolfgang's strength has been a lesson to us all. A strength that emanated from his integrity and genuineness. Though he was not a trained designer, he always placed his common sense and vast legal knowledge at the service of design.

In our international organisation, Wolfgang acted as Treasurer, responsible for ICSID's economics and financing for four intensive years. However, in practice it wasn't enough; he also became actively involved in cultural issues of an international scale, and acted as Account Executive in ICSID-UNIDO negotiations.

His meritorious work leading the Austrian Design Institute and his dedication to the international design community have left behind a legacy and a deep feeling of gratitude for having known him and for having shared memorable moments with him.

His hometown was Vienna, a central lookout on cultural activity. Could it ever have been another city?

Wolfgang Swoboda will always remain in our thoughts.

The new president of the WDO, Miss Luisa Bocchietto, refused to give me official recognition that I was the first in the world, in 1995. (Perhaps the only one) requested this change in the ID definition. I had good reason to insist because most of my design projects were small series products. Ms. Bocchietto presented my proposal to improve the ID definition to the WDO (UO) Board of Directors to include the words: the best compromise, ergonomics and two different product groups, mass and limited produced.

The new president of the WDO, Miss Luisa Bocchietto, refused to give me official recognition that I was the first in the world, in 1995. (Perhaps the only one) requested this change in the ID definition. I had good reason to insist because most of my design projects were small series products. Ms. Bocchietto presented my proposal to improve the ID definition to the WDO (UO) Board of Directors to include the words: the best compromise, ergonomics and two different product groups, mass and limited produced. My proposal wasn't rejected, but that they couldn't apply it at this point. "Right now" may indicate that one day in the future, WDO will include my proposal because these are obviously key words of modern industrial design. That will certainly, to me, remain my legacy to the world's industrial design. No one's ever told me that I talk nonsense.

During the Homeland War, I came to Zagreb and gave lectures and seminars at the Design Study in Zagreb. On this occasion I met Mr. Ivan Doroghy, then president of the Croatian Association of Applied Arts, ULUPUH, who asked me to send him materials of my works created in Europe, the UNITED States and Canada. I sent a package of twelve panels ready for the exhibition. When my package arrived in ULUPUH, the Croatian Law Party by force (arms!) occupied Starčević's building. They threw ULUH and ULUPUH out on the street. Unbelievable savagery!

My wife, just arriving from Canada, tried to save my materials. At the front door, she was greeted by an armed bearded man, and inside the building, a guy with a Nazi salute. She was able to get permission to inspect a basement that was packed with ULUPUH and ULUH stuff. She didn't find anything. That's how I ran out of exhibition materials, but luckily I sent copies of my original panels that I used for presentations in Canada. After that incident, Doroghy never contacted me!

"What I learned in TRS and Prvomajska, I applied it in Canada. I realized I was a typical practitioner. The design theorist is my "counterbalance" which explains my work in a philological way. However, to survive in the world of corporations, there is no room for philosophy My design presentations were always concrete, clear, well-argued, logical solutions, expressed by the vocabulary of engineers, marketing experts and people high up for corporate decisions."

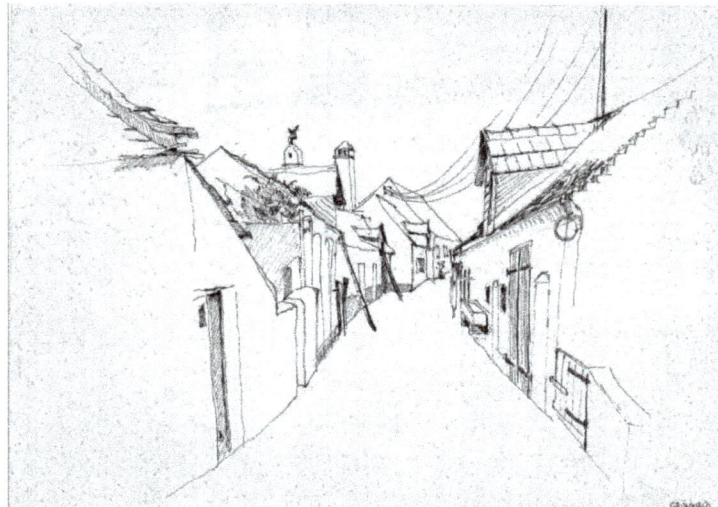

Austria, Burgenland, 1964. D. Grünwald

1976. In Montreal, he worked with Micom on the design of the Micom 2000, personal computer. It was the first computer in Canada and his first design.

1977., he was briefly employed by the Montreal-based company Prodesign, of the same name as his previous Zagreb studio. He designs a folding stand for presentations and utensils

1978., after failed negotiations with Texas Instruments, Grünwald moved to Winnipeg where he got a job with American designer John Vanderhof, where he worked, among other things, on tractor design for Versatile. His concept was accepted because it had a "European look"

*

"After two years in Montreal we had to flee the city because of the political situation, when the Quebecois party led by Rene Levesque came to power, they wanted to secede from Canada. At the time, the treatment of the newcomers was terrible; they wouldn't serve me in the store, the restaurant and the like. And I've just come from another political system that has defined what I can and shouldn't do. I was looking for a way out of that situation, and I found an ad in the paper. Texas Instruments was looking for an industrial designer with European education and experience designing electronic calculators, exactly my description! " I was invited for three days in Dallas, where I had conversations with a dozen department heads. They introduced me to a real estate agent to help me find a house! The last person I spoke to at the end asked me, "Where are you really from?." I replied that I was from Yugoslavia. "Unfortunately, we can't see you," they replied. They were afraid of communist spies. That's when I decided to move to Winnipeg because that's where I got the job."

*

1980., after Winnipeg, Grünwald settled in Toronto, where he got a job as a draftsman at Scintrex, which was involved in the production of geophysical instruments.

1983., he was presented with the prestigious Canada Design Award for Geophysical Instrument Genie, designed for Scintrex a year earlier.

1981. -1984., he works for Delphax on the design of fast printers, corporate identity and exhibition system.

1985., Davor Grünwald was hired by Georics, geophysical company for which he worked on product designs until his retirement in 2008. The vice president, later president and business owner was his colleague, an athlete from the Club Mladost in Zagreb next to Sava river.

From 1990 to 2000, he was vice president of AMCA, an association of alumni of Croatian universities in Toronto. He was responsible for graphic design in GAUDEAMUS.

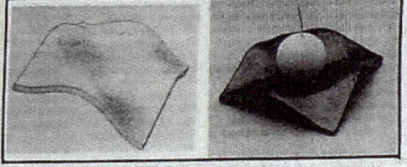

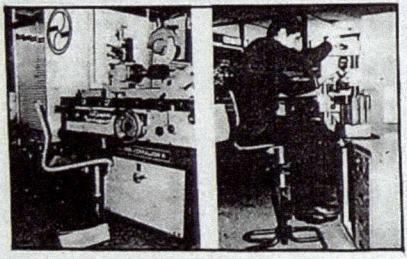

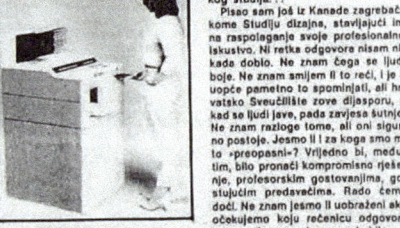

Ana Lendvaj, 1990.

Davor Grünwald , Croatian industrial designer in Diaspora.
The attitude toward design in factories hasn't changed much.
And the Croatian University invites Diaspora, but when people
come forward, there's no answer.

Why is the curtain of silence falling?

Davor Grünwald is a pioneer of Croatian industrial design, who in 1975 became the first formally educated Croatian industrial designer, but he emigrated to Canada. We talk about how the then unfavorable state and social attitude towards the design profession "broke over the back" of the professional despite receiving several significant awards for his design work. Of course, and about today's attitude toward design.

Why exactly you went to Canada in 1975.?

DG: It was a tumultuous time. With a degree from the Vienna Academy of Applied Arts (1968), I came to Zagreb as the first professional graduate industrial designer in Yugoslavia. No one knew me. Two years earlier, the CIO, the Centre for Industrial Design, was founded in Zagreb. The first director was Zvonimir Radić and he was succeeded by Mario Antonini. I was turned down by Antonini's monopolistic attitude, so I turned to my own freelance work. With his unprofessional behavior, very interesting professional impressions, but not solutions, Antonini made me a "favor".... I got jobs in the Factory of Calculating Machinery, then in Prvomajska, machine tools factory, metal furniture factory "Jadran". There's a lot of talk about the fact that before me, unsuccessfully, there was CIO. It turned out that I was doing very well, when it came to business - I set myself competitive. The results were, in 1973, the Award of the City of Zagreb for the machine tools for Prvomajska, the golden plaque at the largeest fair in Leipzig for the same machine tools and the BIO (Industrial Design Biennale) for the electronic calculators of TRS.

Redesign of mech. and design of several electr. calculators, pocket calc. electr. scale,1969.-1974

But in 1974, our "famous" federal government banned all factories from using private services, which I was as a professional freelancer. "Overnight" I lost all contracts, the base for life. I and my family steady income, didn't have an apartment, we were doomed to clear economic emigration and a bit political because the Communists were "running" after me and I refused to sign the application form, which was pretty dangerous. I knew Toronto was a great industrial center, but the first industrial designer, in then Yugoslavia, very quickly faced the reality of "golden America".... Yet after a few non-professional initial jobs, I found my first job in the profession. I became a member of the Professional Association of Industrial Designers of Canada and bit by bit I formed my status... I am now well known in Canada.

Can you describe your student work, an abstract spherical module, for our newspaper readers?

DG: During the first year, during my studies in Vienna, Professor Hoffman gave us a theoretical task, to create a module that, when multiplied, can be connected in a vertical direction and cannot be disassembled in horizontal directions. My solution was based on the multiplication of the two sinus functions, which forms an extremely attractive and harmonious module. It became my three-dimensional emblem.

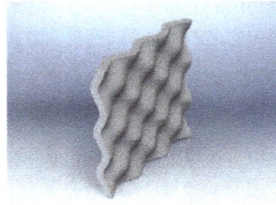

Sculptra module, 1964

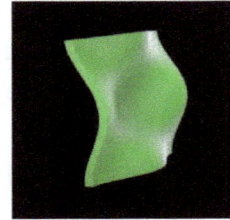

DG: During the first year, during my studies in Vienna, Professor Hoffman gave us a theoretical task, to create a module that, when multiplied, can be connected in a vertical direction and cannot be disassembled in horizontal directions. My solution was based on the multiplication of the two sinus functions, which forms an extremely attractive and harmonious module. It became my three-dimensional emblem. My wife made simple, usable objects from that, in Toronto: an ashtray, a wall plaque, and abstract wall compositions that she gave to the Croatian Embassy and Consulate in Canada.

I and my friend created a mathematical formula with which we used CNC(Computer Numerical Control) milling machine to create a module with a size of 61 x 61 x 15 cm and I called it SCULPTRA, for an architectural application.

What is the common denominator in shaping your products?

DG: It is certainly the purity of form, formal harmony and all subordinate to ergonomic study, technological possibilities, and choice of materials of the product concerned. Industrial design is a rational process, but it also has an irrational/emotional component. It is necessary to have a natural talent and a good, versatile education to bring it all together into a likable product.

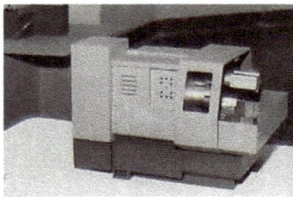

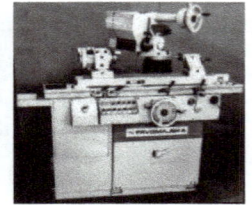

. Redesign of tool machines for Prvomajska, Models in 1:10 scale, 1970. – 1974.

Your ergonomic tests were remembered in your Zagreb career in the 1970s. Please give me examples?

DG: When designing machine tools for Prvomajska, this ergonomic component is explicitly important when working with the machine and maintenance. The command panel must be organized so that the informational display is at eye level and the mechanical commands at the height of the bend hand. Access to the operating portions of the machine must be stress-free and the operator has to have good protection when operating the machine. When designing the machine tools, I noticed that the workers were sitting on wooden boxes when working on machines. It led me to study these circumstances, so I designed the chairs for that purpose. This was spotted by the director of metal furniture "Jadran" and he offered me the position of director of development. I accepted that offer, but that "arrangement" lasted only three months when that same director made a request that I have to join the Communist Party. I didn't accept that. When working on the design of electronic calculators for TRS, I also applied ergonomic conditionality's, from which the formal aesthetic of very original, likeable electronic calculators came out.

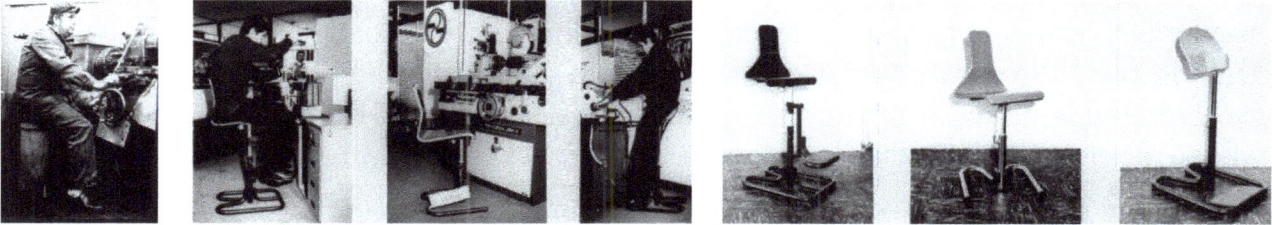

Industrial chairs for Jadran, 1970. - 1972.

What was the relationship between state and society toward design as a profession and a professional calling?

DG: First of all, I must mention that no factory had a "job description" for a designer. The design was considered as an additional cost. That impression probably stemmed from monopolistic, expensive fees CIO offered. Yet with its action, the CIO achieved that factory directors had roughly some idea of industrial design and what they were getting with such treatment. That's why I, with my far smaller fees, have been able to arrange deals and also educate directors what to expect from my (or other designer) engagement. So at the time there was hope that this trend of embracing industrial design in factories would survive. Some advanced factories such as RIZ, Nikola Tesla had a permanent working relationship – architects. The federal government has succeeded in ruin the freelance designers (my case) by banning factories from working with them. It was a colossal (communist) nonsense and that's why I immigrated to Canada.

Have you been following the home design scene in Canada? Will you come back here?

DG: Yes, I followed from a distance. Still, I was focused on survival in Canada and very engaged. I had the impression of a big gap, no progress for the better in Croatia. With the establishment of the Faculty of Design Studies at the Faculty of Architecture in 1989, then the beginning of a free Croatia and then the awakening of the national consciousness – I knew it would take two generations to fall everything into place. A destroyed and weakened industry because of the Homeland War won't be able to employ young industrial designers for much longer, graduates of the Design Study. Healthy industrial design requires a healthy industrial base. And that little industrial base before the Homeland War - it's gone!

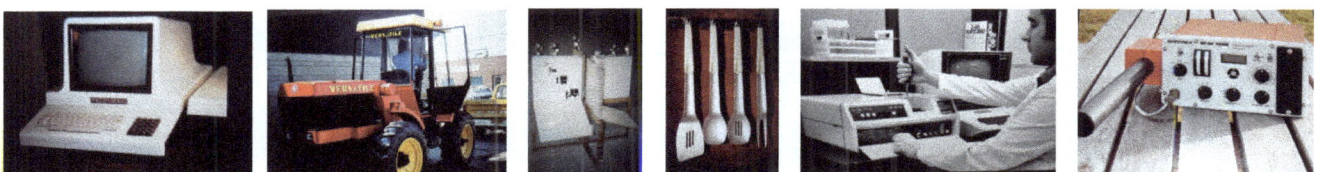

Computer, tractor. folding stand, utensils. Genie geophysical instr. Atomic absorption instr. 1975. – '85.

DG: I wrote to Canada Design Studies, offering my professional experience available to them. I didn't get a line of an answers. I don't know what people are afraid of. I don't know if I can say it, and if it's even a good idea to bring it up, but the Croatian University calls Diaspora, and when people come forward, the curtain of silence falls. I don't know the reasons for that, but they certainly do exist. Are we and who are we too dangerous? It would be worth it, however, to find a compromise solution, to professorial guests, visiting lecturers. We'll be happy to come. I don't know if we're pretentious if we're expecting a few lines of reply to messages, even if the offers have been rejected...   I'll be back in Croatia for sure when I receive the Canadian pension.

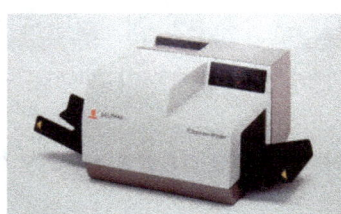

. Fast ion printer: horizontal, vertical – office,   Exhibition system 1980. – 1984.

In 1983, Delphax company headquarters moved from Toronto to Boston and they invited me to join them. One day, the head of marketing invited us to a meeting. He began by asking: "Davor, why did you make a new trademark in red? The traditional American color is blue." I didn't know what to say to him. I told him that he forgot it was still a Canadian company, and the traditional Canadian color is red (flag). And it was Canadian, even though negotiations with Xerox had begun. He blushed (he didn't turn blue!) and rushed out. After that, there was a long tight silence in the room. The next day, I got fired. After two years, I was awarded a large amount of money in damages by the court for expelling me for no valid reason. After that, he was kicked out from Delphax.

Feđa Vukić, 1993.

In the last system domestic savvy was treated as excess
(hi) story: Davor Grünwald, industrial designer

IN THE "SELF-GOVERNING ACTS" OF THE CCMPANIES THERE WAS NO JOB DESCRIPTION OF THE "DESIGNER"
DOMESTIC INDUSTRY WAS MOSTLY BASED ON COPYING AND PURCHASING OUTDATED TOOLS AND MODELS OF THE "WEST"
IN CROATIA, UNFORTUNATELY, NEITHER PEOPLE NOR MENTALITY, NOR HABITS HAVE CHANGED YET.

In Zagreb these days came for a short while Davor Grünwald, a man whose fate is truly marked, could almost say, was shaped by design. He was one of the pioneers of Croatian industrial design, and because of the restrctions imposed on him by the former politiccl system, in 1975. he emigrated to Canada, where he also had a pioneering role and soon broke into the very design peak. In 1983. his work was crowned with the prestigious Canada Design Award.

Davor Grünwald was born in 1943. in Zagreb. After graduating from high school, he enrolled in the Faculty of Electrical Engineering in Zagreb, followed by Akademie fur Angewandte Kunst in Vienna, where he graduated in 1968. in the industrial design department. After graduation, he spent nine months in a residency at the Institute for Industrial Design in Vienna. After returning to Zagreb he began to work professionally as an independent designer and as such collaborated with many Croatian industrial companies: Prvomajs<a, the Factory of Calculating Machines, the Pencil Factory and the Scale Factory. In 1972 he was appointed director of development of the Jadran's Metal Furniture Factory in Zagreb, but after three months he resigned, because as a condition of employment he did not want to accept, membership in the Communist Party. After that, he resumes working in the free profession.

In 1975, after being denied that as an independent designer, he could work for state factories, he immigrated to Canada, where he still lives. These days, after eighteen years of professional denuding, Grünwald reappecred in Zagreb, giving us an ideal opportunity to thoroughly get known his exceptionally rich, interesting and successful design career, one of many Croatian design careers that are almost unknown to our public.

What, at the time you started, so in the late 1960s – in Zagreb there was a "climate" for a young man who, as the first in Croatia, had a degree in industrial design from the Vienna Academy?

D.G. Preparing for my studies, I spoke to Zvcnimir Radić, one of the founders of exact 51 group and then director of the Centre for Industrial Design, CIO in Zagreb. That month ct the Museum of Arts and Crafts, MUO I saw an exhibition of Italian design and I had already made the definitive decision that I simply had to study design. Radić told me: "Unfortunately, in Europe, there is only one valuable school for design – the one in Ulm. And there's something in Vienna." I couldn't get to Ulm because the Germans didn't give me a visa, so I arrived in Vienna and enrolled in the Academy of Applied Arts (Akademie fur Angewandte Kunst), industrial design department. At the end of my studies I was offered to stay in Vienna, but I wanted to return to Zagreb and work for our factories. Besides, I started a family and my daughter was one year old. I had no idea what I could expect in Croatia at the time. I had a poor knowledge of the situation.

I received a scholarship from Croatia for postgraduate studies in Austria. It saved me financially. The first period in Zagreb passed in the exploration of opportunities for work. The question was, "what can I do here?" Clearly, after the stage of initial enthusiasm, there was disappointment, and my great expectations were soon reduced to a realistic (Croatian) measure.
At that time the Center for Industrial Design, the CIO had already changed its director – Zvonimir Radić was replaced by Mario Antonini, and it is logical that as a young designer eager for work, I went there first. However, the first conversation on me left an unfavorable impression because Mario had let me know that the situation was difficult and that there was no work.

After the failed attempt to find a job through the CIO, I tried through the Association of Visual Arts and Applied Arts of Croatia, ULUPUH. I assumed that I would find some like-minded people there, which is what happened: I met colleagues Vladimir Žitković and Antun Karavanić with whom I founded the ULUPUH Industrial Design Section, and later collaborated with them on other projects.

What was the role of the Industrial Design Centre really at the time? How did function one such, beyond no doubt, an important national institution for promoting design?

D. G. My impression back then was that the people at the Center had a theoretically extraordinary, elaborate system, that they had a good way (theoretically) approaches and great presentations, and they had behind them people like Fedor Kritovac, Matko Mestrović and Goroslav Keller, beyond doubt, design theorists of the format. But very quickly I got the impression that it was all they had - I believe they had great presentations but high fees and they behaved monopolistically. I believe, there was no power at the Center itself or in the social environment then at all, to bring the design process to a logical end - to the realization. The CIO as a National Institution for the Promotion of Industrial Design should not have behaved like commercial companies and competed with us freelancers for what few jobs in the industry. But they had political/communist support and they could do whatever they wanted.

Realizing that, I didn't even try to get a job through the Center, but I went with a different strategy. Everywhere the Center failed to make a deal or for some reasons went awry, I, with my formal education, as the first industrial designer, simply performed competitively - as a standalone designer, I could have been much cheaper than the Center, so probably factory directors resonated: "let's try what this kid knows and can do." In this way, I have done relatively quickly the TRS's trademark was really ugly, so I suggested a new one. TRS's new trademark displays the symbolic ruciment of an electro-computer – a binary system with small magnets that TRS's electricians had fun with before they were given transistors. That was the inspiration for that trademark for TRS.

What kind of manufacturers were they?

D.G. The first was the Computer Machinery Factory, TRS. I got to them by accident. They were close to the apartment where I lived, so one day I visited them and offered myself to the director for a job without any recommendation. In the same way, I came to the Prvomajska, machine tool Factory.

TRS were mostly working on mechanical calculating machines at the time. For them, 1969. I redesigned their old CALCOREX 403 and in the same year I created their new trademark.

D. G. This mechanical calculator was produced for about twenty years by the Czech License. It was heavy, cumbersome and the numbers were barely noticeable, the housing of the sheet metal, imprecise. My task was to redesign it to "extend his life" for the next ten years. I suggested to engineers to use thinner metal materials for internal construction (becoming lighter and smaller). I replaced the sheet metal housing with injection orange/red plastic. The black figures were imprinted with a hot process in plastic and were in stark contrast to the red backing (far better visibility). Thus, TRS's mechanical calculator became a small office attraction by extending its 'life' for a further 10 years.

TRS's trademark was really ugly, so I suggested a new one. TRS's new trademark displays the symbolic rudiment of an electro-computer – a binary system with small magnets that TRS's electronic engineers had fun with before they were given transistors. That was the inspiration for that trademark.

At the time, TRS realized that the "West" was developing electronic calculators, so their electronic engineers dealt with a binary system with magnets wrapped in wires. When transistor technology appeared on the market, TRS did not hesitate, began the development of electronic calculators. Having a good experience with me, I was hired to develop the concepts of electronic calculators.

Redesign of mechanical and several electronic calculators for TRS, pocket calc. scale, 1969. – 1974.

At that time, it was undoubtedly avant-garde, or at least a pioneering policy towards the development of its own production and towards design. For TRS, in the period up to 1974, you designed the whole series of office electronic devices and field calculators with distinctive shapes.

D.G. Yes, it was great "refreshment" that TRS behaved so avant-garde. TRS's electricians have mastered transistor technology relatively quickly. They could have given me all the electro components that affected the final form of the product. With my ergonomic studies, I created a retracted screen (to avoid external reflections) which later Olivetti, and Olympia copied, or their designers came up with the same results with design logic. At first I used electronic tubes for screen figures and later it was replaced by digital screens. I am convinced that if TRS had access to the Western market it would have been very successful. But then the politics of Yugoslavia, or conducting economy, focused only on the market of the "eastern bloc".

All this time you've been working as a freelance designer?

D. G. I could not have done otherwise, because no factory had a job description of a "designer" in its "self-governing acts" so that technically it was not possible for me to get a permanent job. But then I did well in my status as an independent artist, so it was absolutely good for me.

You were also working on an electronic scale project in 1974. for the Scale Factory, a company that in its history has been positively oriented towards the role of design in the development process.

D.G. And in this case the CIO was there before me at that company, but they failed to "impose themselves." It was such an easy job for me because the engineers accepted me as a valuable member of the team. I took over the mechanical parts of the scale, added an electronic swivel "head" that could be adjusted to the desired angle of view of the seller and the buyer (ergonomics!). I was able to make a model in the right size. Then that law came out those factories weren't supposed to work with privates and I immigrated to Canada after that, and I don't know what happened to that. I know that company stopped working soon, too.

It was also a sophisticated high-tech product at the time. Who gave the initiative to engage the designer?

D.G. The Initiative came from the factory itself. The scenario was the same as in the other factories I worked for. I've dealt with reasonable, intelligent people who have realized they need my help in designing products to successfully compete in the market. However, they understood and felt that something had to change and they gave the industrial designer the opportunity to come up with a concept and to give them guidelines for the development of a new product that was a lot at the time.
It has often been that the manufacturers simply reject the design services on the grounds that there is only an additional cost for the development. In many cases, I was able to prove

the opposite (in Croatia and Canada), and luckily that was the case because i was able to live off my own work as a freelancer, which was always my intention.

It wasn't easy, though. Because at the same time I was supposed to live my life and work in an educational sense – constantly explaining what industrial design is and what its place is in the product development process. I had to convince people of what I was doing so that they would finally sign me a contract. However, as difficult as all this was, I learned very much in this way because at the same time I had to be everything: author, manager, promoter and educator.

With colleagues Žitković and Karavanić you organized in Zagreb in the early 1970s, annual awards for good design, Yu-design.

D.G. It was an initiative that concerned the entire federation at the time. It was organizationally supported by the ULUPUH Industrial Design Section and called YU - DESIGN. The awards were given in 1972. and 1973. The jury was done at the Zagreb Autumn Fair, because it was simply the most practical – all the producers from Yugoslavia were there. Unfortunately, this initiative has failed to sustain and grow into a tradition. However, such an action implies professional conduct, and all of us involved were at the same time forced to take care of our own daily existence. No one was prepared to support the action from representatives of the institutions of "social interest." The few of us lasted two years and after that everything just stopped. The action had no support from cultural institutions either. In accordance with our intentions, the said action could eventually have grown into an institution of meaning Design Centre in London, but - as it has been shown over time, it was nonetheless too ambitious a plan for our cultural/social standard of the time.

Isn't cultural perception of design a constant problem in Croatia?

D.G. Yes, of course, but it wasn't just that a problem - it was something else. I can say that at that time in the development departments of domestic producers, it was popular to travel around the "West" and look for models of products of different types and uses. They bought cheap licenses and imported old tools for models that were long outdated in the West. Croatia (Yugoslavia) had a privileged status to supply Eastern Europe with such things. When such a method began to be systematically implemented came the end of inventiveness and any chance of success in the Western market. Because of that, designers did not get jobs; it was easier for manufacturers go along the "line of least resistance". This short-sighted method completely destroyed the cultural aspect of the design and because of the belief that design and invention are unnecessary investments. Of course, there were honorable exceptions for which I was fortunate to work.

Was such an exception the Jadran factory when you got engaged there in the early 1970s?

D.G. Yes and no! At the time, "Jadran" was one of the leading companies when it came to investing in its own development, even in design as part of that process. However, they did not miss the stage of buying old models in the West. I remember my first working meeting with the director. He explained to me that i would occasionally go to the West and look for models that they could buy cheaply. I replied that I hadn't invested five years of industrial design studies to "design" in such a way. He didn't bother me with that anymore.

When I was designing machine tools for Prvomajska, I noticed that the workers were sitting on wooden boxes when working with them. It led me to study these circumstances, so I designed the chairs for that purpose. It was spotted by the director of metal furniture "Jadran" and he offered me the position of director of development. I accepted that offer, but that "arrangement" lasted only three months when that same director requested that I have to join the Communist Party. I didn't accept that.

In that short period I managed to secure a scholarship for Mladen Orešić, who studied the same industrial design in Vienna. Today he is a professor of design at the Design Study in Zagreb.

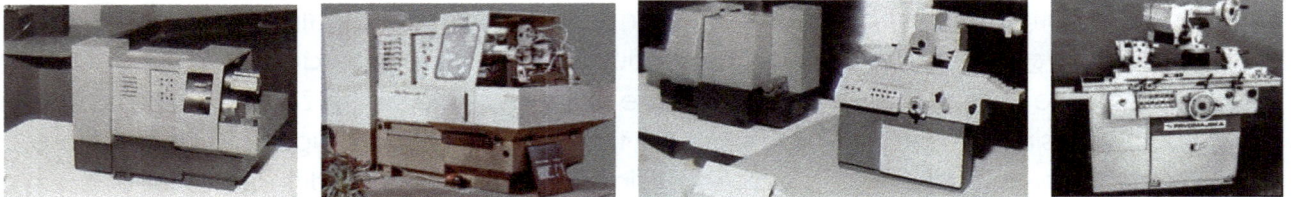

Redesign of tool machines for Prvomajska, Models in 1:10 scale, 1970. – 1974.

You mentioned Prvomajska. What's the story behind it?

D.G. I walked in with them one day as well and offered my design expertise. I started first with the redesign of the automatic sharpener – the Geometric. And then I worked on the automatic grinder 430-431 that was in the development phase. I suggested bases to be made of welded steel plates instead of the cast iron in which they were masters. I've proven that this method is cheaper. I also applied this method to the next redesign of the AT-250 automatic lathe. I organized/designed these machine tools to the maximum and suggested to abound brown Hammerschlag, and instead apply dark brown colour for the bases and light brown for the upper part. I got for those machines in 1973. The City of Zagreb Award and the golden plaque in Leipzig.

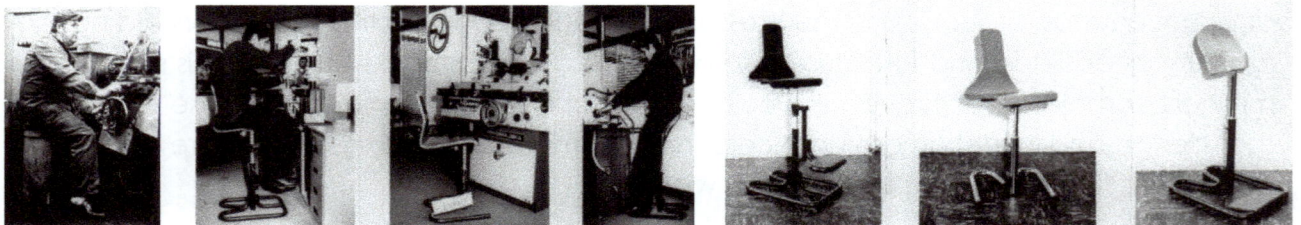

Industrial chairs for "Jadran", 1970. – 1972.

After the "Jadran" fiasco, you became a freelance designer again?

D.G. It was my only choice. There were no job descriptions for "designer". But soon came a new shock - the then federal government in 1974 prohibited state factories to hire private experts. Since I had such status I lost "overnight" all contracts with my clients. Then I found myself in doubt: TRS offered me a permanent employment relationship and an apartment after twenty years of waiting or all of it to leave and immigrate to Canada and "look for a place under the sun" in this democracy, very successful country. I've decided on that challenge!

Why Canada?

 D.G. In moments like that, one thinks quite practically. At the time, the borders were closed in all European countries for which I was interested as a designer. I tried it in Switzerland and then Germany – it didn't work out. I knew it was good to stay in Europe, but the choice was narrowed to what was then possible: Australia or Canada. Australia is really too far away and so the choice has fallen to Canada where I am today.

How quickly did you get there in a professional sense?

D.G. If you think painting balconies and apartments is professional, then I was quick to get by. Joking aside, I got my first design job six months after my initial survival. You know, there's one rule there, when a new immigrant comes in and looks for a job he's been asked the question: Do you have a Canadian experience? It's impossible to answer that question positively: Do you have a Canadian experience, when you first got there, from the other side of the world! The process of "entering" Canadian society is a very complicated and long process if you want to get in a position to do what you want and think you know best.

I was somewhat fortunate to get an engagement relatively quickly in a factory that produced housings for electronic systems. I was asked to fully respond to the demands of my clients, so I sought to make the most of this situation. Yet after six months, I experienced the reality of the democratic system. One day I come to work and I find the door closed – the company collapsed with the death of the owner. Such a shock is certainly great; especially for someone like me who was full of fascination, came from some completely different environment. And since I bought myself a new car from my first incomes – after the collapse of that company, I was unemployed, and I was driving in a new sports car. The state made sure to supply me with a monthly unemployment income that made me survive to the next job.

Would it be possible to define a common thread guide in your design – solutions?

D.G. I WOULD EXTEND THE QUESTION TO MY LIFE PHILOSOPHY. SOMEHOW AT THE TIME OF MY TEENEGER MATURATION, I REALIZED THE IMPORTANCE OF BALANCE IN THE MACRO AND MICRO WORLD. I FELT INTENSELY JIN AND YANG EVEN THOUGH I DIDN'T KNOW OR HEAR ANYTHING ABOUT IT. MY DECISION TO BECOME A DESIGNER WAS COMPLETELY INSTINCTIVE. SO THE TRADEMARK OF MY FIRST CONSULTING COMPANY "PRODESIGN" (FOUNDED IN ZAGREB IN 1969) AND LATER FORBIDDEN BY THE THEN AUTHORITIES, SYMBOLIZED THE IDEA OF ORGANIZING LIMITATION AND IMPERFECTION AND SHAPED TO BRING IT INTO HARMONY AND BALANCE. THUS, THIS TRADEMARK REPRESENTS A CIRCLE – A SYMBOL OF THE IDEAL FORM AND WITHIN IT ALL DESIGN INFLUENTIAL ELEMENTS IN SOME COMPROMISE RELATIONSHIP. THAT WOULD BE MY GUIDING THREAD AND BASIC APPROACH TO EVERY DESIGN TASK, INCLUDING SOLVING LIFE'S PROBLEMS.

. Computer, tractor, folding stand, utensils, Genie geophysical instr. Atomic absorption instr. 1975. – '81.

In Canada, you stayed (continued) in the field of high-tech design, computer terminals, electronic equipment and geophysical devices, so practically – you continued to do the work for which you gained good experience in Zagreb? Can the fundamental differences between the notion and practice of design in Croatia and Canada be highlighted because of your experience?

D.G. That's a large, very good question, because the differences are large as well. Canada is a *democratic society with a century-old tradition, freedom to act within the limits of standard regulars*. My status as a free designer has been stimulated by the state's various tax benefits. Croatia, by the time I left it, was a communist state with politically motivated regulars that made me leave, practically drove me away!

Canada is known as a country rich in raw materials/ores, so the production of capital products is far more developed than those of consumers. They are importing consumer products from the United States and Europe. The raw material processing industry in Canada is authentic. I quickly realized this and in the industry of capital, high-tech products found my place. My experience from Zagreb I could have used to a lesser extent, but more in terms of dealing with people with whom I had to communicate. The geophysical industry in Canada is the strongest in the world and Toronto is the world center of that industry. I have imposed myself on this industry and I have a kind of monopoly and I cover a large segment of the design development of geophysical instruments.

Fast ion printers: horizontal, vertical – office, exhibition system. 1980. – 1984.

It has a small resemblance to Croatia. Canadian corporations, too, didn't know industrial design a decade ago. But they quickly realized and accepted that the design helped them to be competitive on a global scale. The Canadian Professional Association is very aggressively promoting industrial design. This has helped to this matter. I will be immodest and declare that I have contributed to that greatly with my work. This dimension of consciousness in Croatia could not develop due to restrictions of the political system and very little technological influence on the rest of the world.

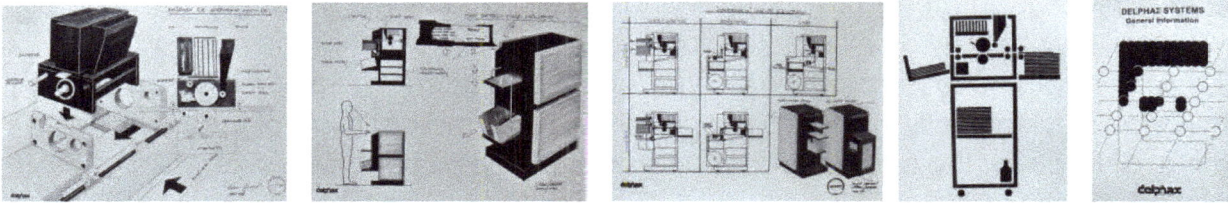

Sketches in connection with development of fast ion printers, 1980. – 1984.

AFTER A VIOLENTLY INTERRUPTED BUT HIGHLY SUCCESSFUL CAREER IN HIS HOMELAND, DAVOR GRÜNWALD IN CANADA REALIZES AS EARLY AS 1976. THE COMPUTER TERMINAL FOR MICOM LTD. FROM MONTREAL, AS A CONTINUITY OF PROFESSIONAL INTERESTS FROM CROATIA. DURING THE 1980S, HOWEVER, IT WAS MOST DEDICATED TO SHAPING INSTRUMENTS AND PRACTICAL AIDS FOR GEOPHYSICAL INDUSTRY (SINCE 1984.) IS A CONSULTANT AT GEONICS LTD. AND HE WORKS WITH OTHER COMPANIES SPECIALIZING IN THE PRODUCTION OF GEOPHYSICAL INSTRUMENTS), SO TODAY HE IS ONE OF CANADA'S LEADING EXPERTS IN THIS FIELD. IT DOESN'T NEGLECT OTHER ELECTRONICS INDUSTRIES EITHER - SINCE 1981. – 1984., HE IS DEVELOPING FOR THE COMPANY DELPHAX A SERIES OF FAST PRINTERS WITH THE THEN NEW ION PRINTING TECHNOLOGY. FOR THE SAME COMPANY IN 1983, HE ALSO CREATED A COMPLETE VISUAL IDENTITY AND EXHIBITION STAND SYSTEM. HE WON THE CANADA DESIGN AWARD IN 1983. FOR DESIGN OF ELECTROMAGNETIC TRANSMISSION AND RECEIVER SYSTEM SE-88 GENIE, FOR EXPLORATION OF CONDUCTIVE MINERALS.

.   Genie, antenna, winch, EM38 and EM61 geophysical instr. Radar geof. Instrument, 1984. – 1994..

Croatia today is not the same as Croatia, which you left in the mid-1970s. Do you see any changes in the design relationship?

D.G. Little has changed, because the economic situation is the same, if not worse. I believe it will take at least two generations to make things better so that awareness of design based on private ownership and a competition-based production initiative, could be changed for the better in Croatia, according to what you said, was design as a cultural fact. However, the fact is that with this Homeland War the industrial base has been destroyed and a healthy base is a prerequisite, that young industrial designers educated at the newly established Design Studio in Zagreb find jobs. I hear this facility trains about two dozen designers a year, which is a hyper production for an industry which hardly exists. I don't understand that math.

Do you think it will be enough to make two generations biologically modified, or will some initiatives be needed in that regard now?

D.G. People, arguably, need to change, and that's probably the hardest thing. Even if in some key positions they didn't stay the same people the fact is that the mental and behavioral habits have remained the same – nothing has changed here. Although I must admit that, staying briefly in Zagreb in April 1991, I felt some optimism of change and a glimmer of hope for the future that has been clearly wiped out by the war.

There is also a much-present problem of the Diaspora, because it is often propagated by the return of our people with professional and financial capital to Croatia, but on the practical level of realization of this idea there are a lot of misunderstandings.

Personally, as a designer from the Diaspora, I would also have to decide - which is not at all easy if you have well established working elsewhere - about possibly returning one day, but the question is whether at the moment when a healthy economic base is finally created in Croatia, I will still have the strength to do the way I I am doing now. So return is a big question. It is clear that the war situation makes it difficult and prolongs the period necessary for the transformation towards the developed economy and so on the different design status in Croatian culture, but it does not mean that at the project level some ideas for the future cannot be worked out already. If there is a need and desire for my engagement in this regard, I will be honored to help.

Century of Croatian Design, Feđa Vukić, 1996. (Excerpt)

.... Exhibitions and awards Produkt – Design, 1971 – 72. (Yu-design) showed a clear aspiration to renew the interests of the society towards design and design problems, but this renovation did not occur at the level of standardization of the need for design. However, some examples - both authors and production companies - testify to the existence of awareness of design and even the possibilities of local context when investors/manufacturers and designer creations are happily joined. The example of the Factory of Computers, Machines from Zagreb is very good in this regard because the company during the 1970s and slightly less in the 1980s invested quite a bit of funds in its own development, So the continuous engagement of Davor Grünwald resulted in a whole series of highly successful electronic table, electronic calculators that were largely assembled from the imported components. The designer's task was to perfect the existing mechanical calculator (Calcorex 403), the development of some individual components (keyboard) and final shape of the machine. During that time it was undoubtedly the pinnacle of the technological power of Croatian industry, which for the company itself created a very favorable market position during the 1970s......

.... An interesting contribution to the involvement of designers is made during the 1970s and 1980s, the company "Prvomajska", for which at the time some projects were done by Davor Grünwald (Prize of the City of Zagreb), Egon Paraker and finally Jasenka Mihelčić. These are mainly industrial lathes and similar machines in which designers mainly solved the problem of machine relationship – server, as well as server protection in the process of operation.....

.... The metal furniture company "Jadran" from Zagreb tried to introduce the design as a standard development strategy with the permanent high ring of Davor Grünwald as director of development. However, this engagement was short-lived, because one of the conditions for this post was membership of the Communist Party, which Grünwald himself did not accept, and after three months he left "Jadran". During the short-term collaboration, Grünwald designed chairs for machinery servers in the industry. These chairs, which have never been mass serially produced, are a very good example of high ergonomic criteria in the foundation of a design concept....

...... In addition to its collaboration with the Factory of Computer Machines , Grünwald worked for the company IVIS in 1974. He designed an electronic scale, and shortly thereafter went to Canada, where he still lives, developing his business in the full sense, just as much as he wanted in Croatia, but there was no possibility. During the 1980s Grünwald specialized in the design of the equipment for geophysical research, and his design of the visual identity of the company "Delphax" was very successful, the stand for fairs, as well as the design of fast computer printers for the same company ....

In 1997, the World Congress of Industrial Designers, ICSID, was held in Toronto. Personally, I was very engaged and organized an exhibition of Canadian industrial designers. On this occasion, I gave a presentation of the works of colleagues and my own projects, such as a mine detector. At the time, the Princess of Wales, Lady Diana, was leading an international campaign to curb land mine production. I sent her a letter on June 1, 1997. and asked for her support, which she did on June 17, 1997. Sadly, on July 30, 1997, she tragically died.

Of course, it was an opportunity to mention Serbian aggression, their rampage and destruction in Croatia, ethnic cleansing and crime against humanity. (Dubrovnik, Vukovar, Srebrenica). I helped two graduates of design from Zagreb get by in Canada. Shortly after arriving in Canada, I became one of the directors of the Canadian Association of Industrial Designers, right up until my retirement.

Burgenland, Austria, 1964. D. Grünwald

Continuity problem – Davor Grünwald
One example of design possibilities in Croatia
Feđa Vukić, 2000. (Excerpt)

.... In such a situation, those few individuals who have engaged in industrial design in Croatia come to the profession with degrees in architecture, electrical engineering or other technical faculty, or, depending on the possibilities, have attended design studies abroad.

In such circumstances, it is not surprising that the history of Croatian industrial design is characterized by a lack of continuity, both in institutional and individual terms. The example of Zagreb designer Davor Grünwald is very instructive in this sense, since it is one of our most active designers who in the late 1960s and early 1970s operated in the field of high-tech products, such as electronic calculators, electronic scales and industrial machines. Grünwald acquired expertise in Vienna, so that he could apply this knowledge in Zagreb for six years, until he was forced to leave the country and move to Canada. It is a problem of ideology indication, certainly not lonely in the history of Croatian industrial design.
In 1975.,he left for economic reasons (due to the legal abolition of the possibility to work as a freelancer for large economic systems) to Canada, where he still lives today.

1980. – 1984. he doesn't neglect another electronics industry, developing for the company Delphax a series of fast ion printing machines. In 1983, for the same company, he developed complete visual identity and fair exhibition system.

In 1983 he was awarded the Canada Design Award for the design of the electromagnetic geophysical system (transmitter and receiver) SE88 GENIE, intended for research of conductive minerals, by Scintrex.

In 1993, after almost two decades of absence from the Croatian cultural scene, he participated in a competition for the visual identity of Slavonska Banka. Davor Grünwald still lives and works in Toronto.

From 1990. - 1994. collaboration with Sensors & Software.

From 1990. – 2008. cooperation with Gem Systems.

2008. Davor Grünwald retires, but continues to work in design.

D. Grünwald - A message to young designers: "A clear, well argument of your approach or concept will convince even the most stubborn that you are right and should listen to you. When I think about all my conflicts with employers today, and there were a lot of them, I would do the same thing. When it all adds up, it's worth it. Towards the end of my career, a member of the company's board in front of the workers called me a shithead and an old fart. I threatened to sue for harassment. The company offered me $100,000 not to sue them. I said yes!"

In September 2015, I was invited to give my professional opus to the archives of the Museum of Arts and Crafts, MUO in Zagreb, on the recommendation of Boris Ljubičić, a world-renowned graphic designer. For me it is a great honor because I return to this Croatian temple of applied art after half a century, in which there was an exhibition of Italian design that inspired me for the future profession. 'This is me" is now a famous chant.

2017. on 3. /09. /'17 – 13./10./'17 an exhibition was held in HDD gallery: **Davor Grünwald : Retrorama of industrial design 1968. – 2008**. As part of the exhibition, a Small Monograph, Davor Grünwald: Industrial Design, with texts by Marko Golub and Koraljka Vlajo, was also published.

Davor Grünwald: Retrorama industrial design 1968 – 2008.

Croatian Design Society, HDD offered to set up an exhibition in September 2017. in their Gallery. The head of the Gallery, Marko Golub, and Koraljka Vlajo, curator of design at the Museum of Arts and Crafts, MUO, have accepted the work of the curators of the exhibition. They were joined by Barbara Blasin, a specialist in setting up the exhibits and graphic designer. The exhibition was very well visited and the media, TV, magazines and newspapers conveyed this extraordinary cultural event.

Daniel Maksymiuk, Canadian Ambassador, speaks at the opening of the exhibition in September 2017

Thank you to the Croatian Design Association for inviting me to be present this evening, and to express my congratulations to HDD, to the curators, and especially to Davor Grünwald for the achievement that this exhibition represents.

I have enjoyed learning about Mr. Grünwald's professional accomplishments, and his contribution to the field of industrial design both here in Croatia and in Canada. In fact, as I understand it, the field of industrial design -- in the way that Mr. Grünwald practices it barely existed in Croatia when he began his career. He had an ambition, a passion, and he pursued it in the place that was at that time the international center of excellence in design.

He brought all that he learned, together with his entrepreneurial drive, back to Zagreb and in a short time established himself and won recognition. It is perhaps easier to imagine this today, with Croatia being an EU member and the world being completely connected. When he did this, it was a true adventure. I wish we all had this courage to pursue our dreams, go out into the world to find something new, and then the determination to apply it and make our own country more successful.

I regret to say that conditions in Zagreb at that time, in the early 1970s, were not entirely conducive for Mr. Grünwald, or for many independent entrepreneurs and innovators. He attained professional recognition, but he also encountered obstacles.

In this way, he migrated to Canada, like so many talented people from this part of the world, and as 300,000 new Canadians from around the world do every year to this day.

And in Canada, as I understand it, he found once again that his field was in its infancy, and he played a direct role in transforming industrial design in Canada from something that happened inadvertently, by accident, by amateurs, into a discipline, a profession, recognized as indispensable by leading Canadian companies. Thank you, Mr. Grünwald, for bringing your talent, and the new techniques you learned in Austria and perfected in Zagreb, and sharing them with your new country.

I am grateful to all the Croatian-Canadians, who have contributed knowledge, talent, energy and innovation and helped to build the open and prosperous country that I have the honor to represent. There are now close to 300,000 Canadians of Croatian heritage, each with their own individual story.

I am grateful to Mr. Grünwald, that through his efforts Canadian scientific instruments, industrial equipment, and many other devices are easier to use, safer, and more pleasant to look at. Thank you, even more, for being such a dynamic and creative member of your new community and your new society.
 Today, Canada and Croatia are friends and partners. Today, Croatia is a country that values entrepreneurship and excellence. There are more and more examples of cooperation in scientific research, trade, investment -- and also industrial design -- that are genuinely two-way. We are lucky that more and more Croatian-Canadians are able to keep one foot on each side of the Atlantic, and to enjoy professional success in both countries.
So I hope that all those who visit this exhibition, in addition to learning about Davor Grünwald and his work, and perhaps learning something new about what makes a successful design, will also be reminded of the many connections, the growing number of connections between Canada and Croatia, the rich and deep relationship that we owe to so many Croatian-Canadians, of whom Davor Grünwald is a remarkable example.

Dobro Dosao u Zagrebu, Gospodin Grünwald. Cestitam. Hvala puno.
(Welcome to Zagreb, Mr. Grünwald. I congratulate you. Thank you very much.)

Davor Grünwald and Danijel Maxymiuk, Canadian Ambassador

PIONEER OF DESIGN IN INDUSTRY

Interview, Davor Grünwald on the occasion of the exhibition in the Croatian Society of Designers From the most famous calculator in the former Yugoslavia to the trunk for his own Porsche

Writes Patricia Kiš,   **JUTARNJI LIST**   **September 2017.**

Davor Grünwald

Calcorex 403

Porsche Boxster rack

Davor Grünwald's exhibition at the Gallery of the Croatian Design Society, HDD, prepared by Koraljka Vlajo and Marko Golub, is one of a series of exhibitions that look at the names behind industrial design in the former Yugoslavia when the authors did not sign separately but the design was considered a joint work. The research revealed the names of the designers behind the design of the porcelain Jugokeramika (those "flowers" admired by Tito with Jovanka), Marija Kalentić who made cosmetics Neva, etc.

Redesign of mechanical & several elec. calculators designs, pocket calk., elec. scale,1969.–'1974.

Davor Grünwald graduated from the Academy of Applied Arts in Vienna, and is the first trained industrial designer in this area. During his career he collaborated with the Factory of Calculating Machines (TRS), Prvomajska, machine tools, Jadran – metal furniture factory and TTM scale factory, all companies have a significant place in the history of Croatian industrial design but all disappeared in post-transition. He designed, among other things, a series of electronic calculators, machine tools and chairs to work with machines.

Redesign of machine tools for Prvomajska, models 1 : 10, 1970. – 1974.

For the design of the machine tools for Prvomajska 1974., as a thirty-year-old and then the youngest laureate, he was awarded the City of Zagreb Award. But he soon left Zagreb and went to Canada, where he has lived for the past 42 years, and where he designed various objects, from acclaimed tractors, computer console (the first in Canada) and other technological gadgets. In Canada, he collaborated with Versatile, Scintrex, Delphax, Sensors & Hardware, Geonics, Gem Systems..... One of his most famous works originated back in the former Yugoslavia was the mechanical calculator Calcorex 403, it was his first order, after graduation, and the last works he designed, the trunk for the Porsche and the chair Ellips.

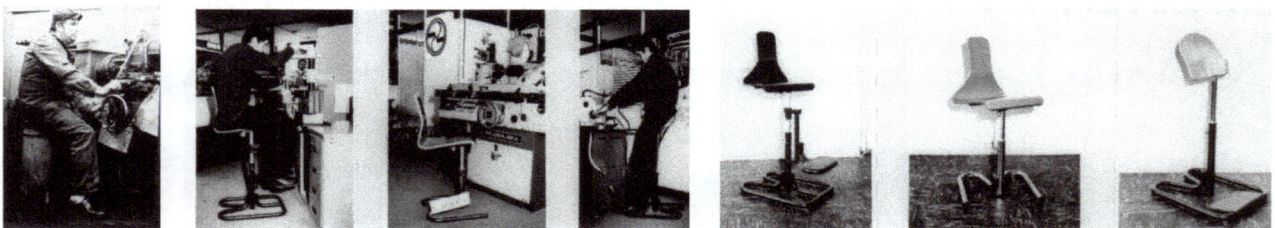

Industrial chairs for "Jadran" , 1970. – 1972.

The authors of the exhibition offer an interesting interpretation of this designer's work: "Looking at everything he has realized, the key common denominator is the sight of a man united with technology, operating heavy machine tools..." We talk about everything with Grünwald, who remembers precisely every moment of his long career.

Computer, tractor, folding stand, utensil, Genie geophysical instr. Atomic absorption instr. 1975.– '81.

You studied electrical engineering first, but in the middle of your studies you went to Vienna to study industrial design. How did it come to this?

D.G. I went to see an exhibition of Italian industrial design that opened at the MUO in 1963. Various products, household appliances, ceramics, plates, etc. were on display and I felt that's what I wanted to do. It was a very intense feeling that I rarely felt in my life. In the immediate vicinity was the Centre for Industrial Design (CIO) where I went to talk to the then director Zvonimir Radić . He told me that the study I want exists in Germany, Ulm and there's something in Vienna. I sat on my Vespa and went to Vienna. I was greeted by Professor Franc Hoffmann, head of industrial design at the Academy. He told me to come in the fall and prepare the materials for the entrance exam. I drove Vespa around Burgenland and sketched and made several usable items. In the fall, there were 30 candidates, I was one of five accepted. It wasn't easy to support myself, I got various jobs in the evenings or weekends like, I worked at the Vienna Opera. It was also a life school. I finished my studies with a high great.

Fast ion printers: horizontal, vertical, office - exhibition system, 1980. – 1984.

You are saying that you've been driving around on Vepa all along. So the love of Italian design was present from a young age?

D.G. These forms always fascinated me, so I designed this way where I could. A good example is my spherical form of Sculptra.

You're going back to Zagreb as the first trained industrial designer?

D.G. Yes, that's exactly how I introduced myself to factory executives. I was cheap and was getting jobs. I was acting capitalistically/competitive. The engineers listened to me. For example, the sharpener was designed as man silhouette!? I suggested using a welded thick sheet metal instead of a cast iron in the sand, which was cheaper. I designed several machines for them, for which I received the City of Zagreb Award and the golden plaque in Leipzig.

Genie, antenna, winch, EM38 and EM61 geophysical instr. Radar geof. Instrument, 1984. – 1994..

For that Bernardo Bernardi praises you for?

D.G. Bernardi wrote that this area of complicated machine tools was not mastered from the shaping aspect from anybody, but I did it! In an era when Richter and Bernardi designed chairs in wood that looked nice and were comfortable to sit on, I designed chairs for machine workers.

How did the Calcorex 403 mechanical computer come about?

D.G. Calcorex 403 has been produced under the Czech License for a number of years. Suddenly he stopped selling, so the TRS director hired me "to extend the life of that machine." Calcorex was heavy, cumbersome, the numbers couldn't be read, the housing made from imprecise sheet metal. I suggested that engineers replace heavy inner metal parts with thinner once, make the casing of sprayed plastic in red and that the black numbers should be applied with hot procedure to the plastic. This made Calcorex smaller, lighter and ergonomically much better. The red color brought vibrancy to the office gray.

Geophysical "bird"　　　Wine barbell　　　Elips chair　　　Control unit

How did you become a director?

D.G. Director of the "Jadran" noticed in Prvomajska my chairs for operators with machines. He invited me to an interview and offered me the position of director of development. After three months, he conditioned me to accept membership of the Communist Party. I refused and I turned around and got out of the "Jadran"! And I went back as a freelance. In the mid-1970s the government of Yugoslavia came out with a law that factories should not use services from free professionals. I lost "overnight" my contracts with all the clients. I immigrated to Canada, where for the first six months; I painted flats and mowed the grass until I found my first job in the design profession.

There, among the many objects you designed a tractor?

D.G. It was in Winnipeg; the agreement was that each of the employees (3) of John Vanderhof consulting would develop their own tractor concept. The CEO of Versital decided on my concept because he has a European touch

   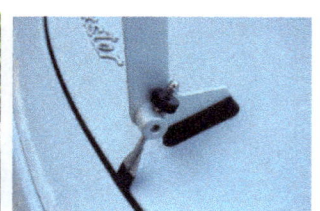

Porsche Boxster rack, 2013.

What are you working on now?

D.G. I decided to have fun with objects without an industrial background. When I retired, I rewarded myself with a Porsche-Boxster. I find out that I can't transport a basket of fruit or antique furniture when my wife and I go on a cruise. I designed the trunk rack I'm putting together in the garage and selling it to my Boxster colleagues. So I sold one on the road in Zagreb! I also designed the chair Ellips: Must have all functions; comfortable to sit on, ergonomicaly, aesthetically correctly and that can be easily produced. But all this with minimal materials and no investment in tools. Production is based on CNC (Computer Numerical Control) technology when making wooden ellipses and metal parts; milling and bending of the Stainless Steel rod. No screws, no welding, no additional hardware and no investment in tools in 2017.

On 15 December 2017. he was awarded with the ULUPUH's Lifetime Achievement Award under the auspices of the City of Zagreb Assembly.

Lifetime Achievement Award, 2017

On the suggestion of Goroslav Keller, ULUPUH awarded D. Grünwald the Lifetime Achievement Award. The award was presented to him by Andrija Mikulić, president of the City Assembly, and Ivana Bakal, president of ULUPUH. This is certainly in the spirit of ULUPUH's mission to reward and stimulate Croatian applied art.

Speech by Davor Grünwald while receiving ULULUH's Awards, November 2017.

Allow me to first welcome and thank you on behalf of all the awarded, Mr. Andrew Mikulić, President of the City Assembly, and Mrs. Ivana Bakal, President of the ULUPUH, in my case for the award of this prestigious ULUPUH Grand Prize for lifetime achievement, as well as for giving the awards to colleagues for the projects presented here, more than successful, projects.

It is certainly in the spirit of ULUPUH's mission to develop, reward and stimulate Croatian applied art. I also welcome all colleagues and friends and family members and all of you who have come to share with us this sense of achievement that this occasion brings with it. You helped us, cheered us on these creative processes of ours that brought us to this today.

I met Mrs. Ana Lendvaj in 1988. when she interviewed me for an article in Večernji list en titled "Why the curtain of silence falls". I am immensely glad to have found myself in her company today, sadly posthumous. I'm sure I share that feeling with everyone. I hope that these awards and everything that has preceded them will contribute to a general, better understanding of industrial, fashion, exhibition and ceramic design creations, and the encouragement of young members and the promotion of honorary members, to properly reveal their artistic maturity. This will ultimately be reflected in the economic, social and cultural development of Croatia. And finally, I want to thank you once again on behalf of the winners – The city hall and ULUPUH for these valuable prizes.
THANK YOU, EVERYONE!

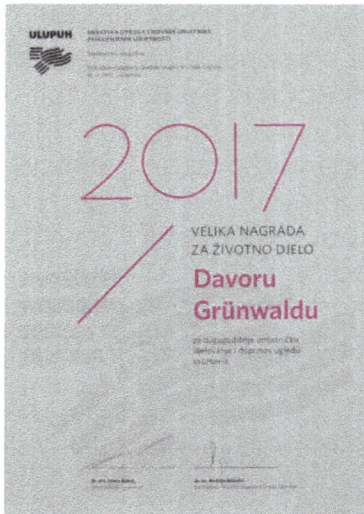

Andrija Mikulić, Davor Grünwald, Ivana Bakal Photo: Morana Matković

*

In half a century of my professional work, a large number of industrial design projects have accumulated. It can be divided into several groups: During the study in Vienna (1964 – 1969), Zagreb phase (1969 – 1875), Canadian phase (1975 – 2008), stage after retirement (2008 – present). It was important to me to show each project in detail: The description of the company, under what circumstances the design originated and what were its main characteristics. In the third year of the study, I designed a "Mechanical Machine for Measuring Anthropological Data" for application in ergonomic analyses. Of course that was before the computer and the laser. From there is generated my "obsession" with ergonomics.

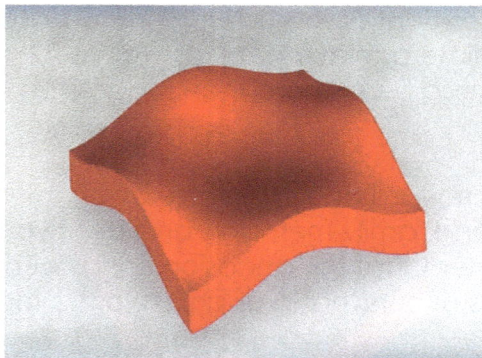

Sculptra pictures   Experiment with the soup

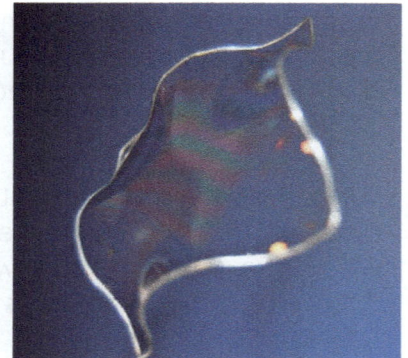

Sculptra, 1964.

"Sculptra is not subject of industrial design, I have never claimed it. It's the only abstract sculptural form I've made in my career. In the second semester, Professor Hoffmann gave us the task of inventing an element that can multiply and connect in a vertical direction (Z) and cannot be broken down in horizontal directions (X,Y). We could use the material and technology of our choice – an ingeniously conceived task! I struggled some time in front of a blank paper, I didn't know where to start. Then, out of desperation, I started thinking about sinusoids and cosine, thanks to the knowledge in mathematics I gained at the Faculty of Electrical Engineering. I was a very good mathematician. So I started playing and I don't know if it was randomly or intentionally, I got that form. Today, I think it was the result of my strong intuition. . All the other student solutions were squarish and in wood, and I came with a curved cast in an epoxy. At the time, there was no computer to prove that this form has no free space when it is assembled. Later, with a mathematical formula, created by a professor at electro-engineering, I proved it. I later portrayed this object and this method of approach as something that represented me as an author, as my three-dimensional trademark. In 1965. at the Museum of Arts and Crafts (MUO) in Zagreb, an exhibition of New Tendencies 3. was staged. I participated with a dozen Sculptors in various colors of 12 x 12 centimeters. After the exhibition ended, I came to pick up my exhibit, but I was told it had been stolen."

"In 1964, there was something about the computers from a distance, and I knew that one day I would be able to process Sculptra with a computer. 1990. with the help of a friend, we created a complicated mathematical formula which we put in the CNC (Computer Numerical Control) milling machine and produced a 61 x 61 x 12 cm (2' x 2' x 5") model, master. SCULPTRA form is abstract, simple. attractive, natural and positive. It looks fresh, as if it was created now and is not a subject to any trends. It will remain unique and eternal in the world! The contrast of light and shadow on its rounded surfaces captures the view of the observer and their interest in this exceptional design." This module has acoustic characteristics – the sound is dispersed on all sides. On the wire frame in the form of SCULPTRA module the soap membrane will form the smallest surface. The name SCULPTRA was created so I left out the second "U" from SCULPTURA and now I could protect that name and the idea remained that it was some kind of sculpture.

Sculptra's first application, 2020   **56 years after conception in 1964**.

Boutique Camping Bunja is a new camp in a pine forest next to the beautiful pebble beach Babin Laz, 2 km from Supetar on the island of Brac, Croatia. The wall separating the sanitary facilities from the camp is lined with 280 Sculptras. Sculptra's wavy form fits perfectly into this seaside setting.

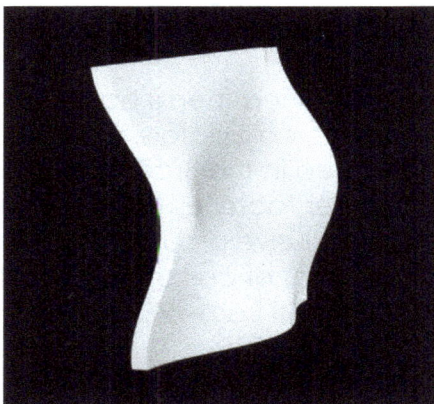

SCULPTRA, architectural module, 2020.

I created this form in 1964. (Davor Grünwald), then a student of the first year of Industrial Design at the Academy of Applied Arts in Vienna. The original size was 12 x 12 cm. This size of 61 x 61 x 15 cm (2' x 2' x 1/2') was made with the help of a CNC (Computer Numerical Control) machine after a mathematical formula that the machine "understood" was developed.

SCULPTRA form is abstract, simple, attractive, natural and positive. It looks fresh, as if it was created now, and not subject to any trends. SCULPTRA confirms the natural phenomenon that between the frame the surface occupies the lowest possible value. The sinusoidal frame will form a soap membrane in the form of SCULPTRA. The contrast of light and shadow on its rounded surfaces captures the view of the observer and their interest in this remarkable design.

The architectural module is made of 2mm thick fiberglass. The matte surface, necessary for maximum contrast of light and shadows, stems from a tool that is thus treated (no additional treatment modules, painting and the like). A type of fibreglass is used that has no smell and does not burn, which is especially important for use in interiors. The weight is about 1.5 kg. Two aluminum "L" profiles are glued to each other for a non-standing installation on the wall or ceiling. If insulation is required, it can be mounted under the module. This form has acoustic qualities – the sound is dispersed on all sides.

The way of preparing the base (wall or ceiling) for the installation of Sculptra modules and the way of mounting Sculptra modules on the wall or ceiling is elaborated and verified on the project "Camp Bunja". Potential clients will receive information about companies that have successfully participated in this project.

I offered Sculptra to the Museum of Contemporary Art (MSU) in Zagreb to store and display it. MSU's director, Ms. Snježana Pintarić declined and commented: "We are not interested in your Sculptra proposal because it does not fit the priorities and strategy of collecting the MSU fondues." The future will say that Mrs. Pintarić is very wrong! It took her four years to send me that answer!

TRS – Factory of calculating machines

Factory of calculating machines, Zagreb was founded in 1948. Since then it has produced measuring instruments for medicine, mechanical and electronic calculators, mini calculators and other calculating equipment. The factory plant was located in the Brače Kavurića street (now Hebrangova Street) in Zagreb. In addition to several other factories (among them: Digitron, PEL Varaždin, Ivasim), TRS belonged to a small and exclusive group of pioneering companies in Yugoslavia that were engaged in the development of calculators. In the design of his products, TRS engaged the designer Davor Grünwald from 1969 to 1975. The factory was shut down in the 1990s.

"I've done electronics before, I've done two-way and three-way radios, and I studied briefly at the Faculty of Electrical Engineering before discovering that I wanted to study industrial design. That (electronics) sensibility never left me. Almost all the industrial design I did later was tied to electronics, and the fact that I had the knowledge and predispositions certainly helped me as a designer. For example, I knew how to talk to engineers, and that's why I've never had a problem here. In both Zagreb and later in the Toronto period, everything was always about electronic devices. The first one I started working with was the TRS that produced electronic calculators, although I did not enter into this cooperation with any particular idea that I wanted to commit to this area. It was a coincidence that TRS was close to my place of residence. Without notice, I walked out on Vodnikova street to Braće Kavurića Street and said, "I'd like to talk to director"

Trade Mark of the Factory of Computing Machines, 1970.

"They've already started producing electronic calculators, so I envisioned the trademark as something that connects to electronics, computer rudiment – binary system with small magnets. It's one of my most successful trademarks. TRS's electronic engineers , before they got transistors, had fun with such binary methods. That's what I saw, and that's how I came up with the idea of a trademark."

Redesign of mechanical calculator, Calcorex 403, 1969.

"The original Calcorex, made by the Czech License, was heavy, the figures could not read, the sheet metal housing was imprecise. A few weeks after I joined the company, I brought sketches with improvements. I suggested thinner metal components making Calcorex smaller and lighter. I further suggested a housing made of injected plastic and the black numbers was imprinted with a hot procedure. From the very beginning, the housing was red so the "gray" office table would little "revive." They accepted it all without a hitch, the redesign of the mechanical Calcorex was created, which extended the life of this product line by ten years, which was the basic task of redesigning. Like all other companies, they sold their products in the Eastern Bloc. It all went to Russia, Czech Republic, Hungary, etc. At the time of the redesign of Calcorex, TRS decided to develop electronic calculators. They hired a couple of electronic engineers and hired me to work on concepts with them. Since they had a good experience with me by development of Calcorex they had full trust in me.

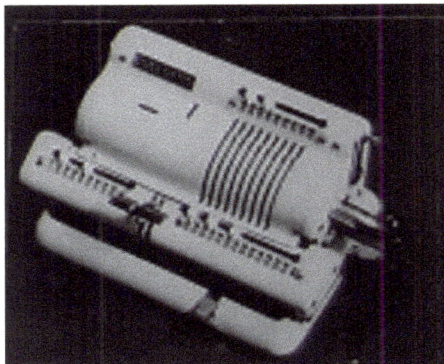

Old Calcorex

New Calcorex

Electronic Table Calculators (1970 - 1974)

Immediately after the completion of my industrial design study in Vienna (1969) I got a contract job for the Factory of Calculating Machines, TRS in Zagreb. At that time the transistor technology was available, so a TRS decided to develop ELECTRONIC TABLE CALCULATORS. They had a secure market behind the iron curtain, the Eastern Bloc of Communist countries including the large Russian market. At the same time the big companies of the West and Japan: SHARP, TOSHIBA, CANON, ADLER, CASIO, OLYMPIA, TEXAS INSTRUMENTS, all developed electronic desktop calculators. But all these products were ugly as if companies didn't know about industrial design. I recently found these vintage products on the Internet and confirmed this fact. Based on this I can state that my design of electronic table calculators for TRS in the early 1970s was very advanced.

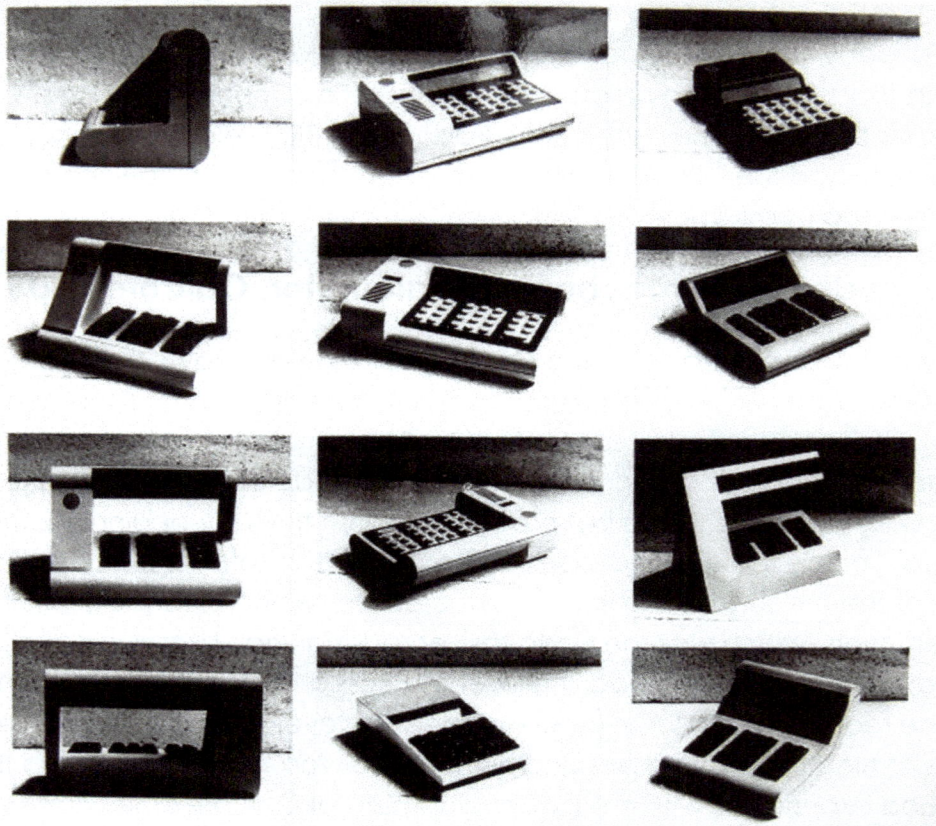

Study of formal design possibilities of electronic calculators for TRS, 1970.

Based on my study of electronic components and ergonomics, the original concept came up with a recessed screen. None of the companies mentioned above had that in the early 1970s. Some later copied it.

TRS501, Electronic, table calculator, 1971.

'TRS501 stemmed from a study of variations in formal possibilities with electronic components with which the TRS electronic engineers then in 1970. were able to use. It was important for me to come up with the concept of strong ergonomic characteristics. I noticed that the desktop (with keys) must have a slight slope for easier access to the keyboard, and I concluded that the display must be indented to avoid environmental reflections.

I couldn't match those findings with the calculators of Western companies - which information just wasn't there. I later found out that these were unique solutions based on my analysis of pure ergonomics, and that was always my strong suit.

TRS501

TRS527 / INDEX, battery calculator, 1973.

The TRS marketing service has seen the need for a smaller, portable version of an electronic calculator powered by batteries. The characteristic novelty of this design was that I attached all the components to the middle PC panel, and the lower and top cover were cheap y made in injection plastic. Another advantage of this concept was that the calculator could be adjusted before the final closing. Here I am using first time my original keyboard design, because in the case of TRS 501 keyboards were purchased ready-made. You will notice that all the buttons have a prominent cylindrical shape on a square basis and that the upper surface is countersank – tactile feedback tells you that you are in the middle of the button. This avoids errors that occur by accidentally pressing the adjacent button. At the time, I expected that my this keyboard design would be copied by someone because it was ergonomically justified. However, since Yugoslav products were not present in the western market, that didn't happen. It is significant that TRS has decided to develop its keyboard on my initiative".

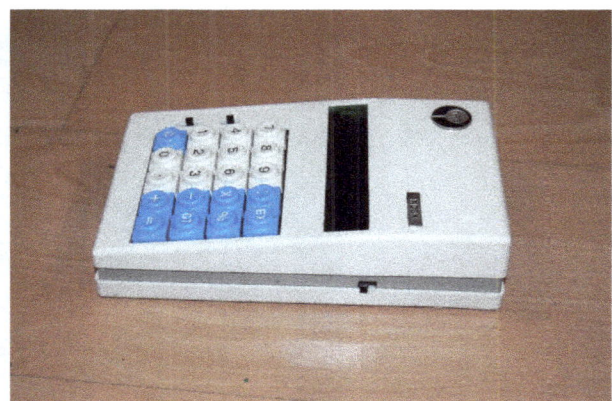

TRS527

TRS533, Electronic, table calculator, 1974.

"This concept was present in the cardboard models of variations of the possibilities that I made in 1970," I wondered why such a device must be symmetrical in the first place? With the design of this calculator, I wanted to explore the advantages of an asymmetric concept, namely, large components such as transformers and capacitors dictated taking work surface of the office table, so I placed them on the side of this model. This approach provides a larger workspace in front of the calculator. The keyboard is my original, square one with a cylindrical upper part, since it has proved very successful with the battery calculator INDEX

TRS533, green

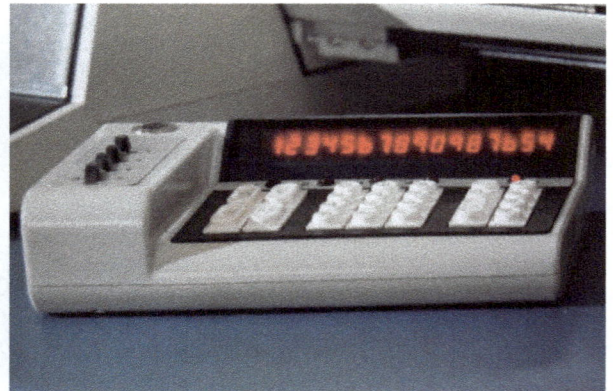

TRS533, white

Pocket calculator Minilog 37, 1969. (Independent project)

I was hired by a Zagrebian who had a small company of electronic products in Germany. I don't remember how he got to me. In Munich, we agreed on all the terms of my engagement. At the time in Europe, no one was producing pocket calculators. But that man was meddling, he never paid me for my design. I didn't want to deal with him anymore, so I don't know how that story ended. And for his company Elmico I developed a trademark (on the pocket of the model blouse"

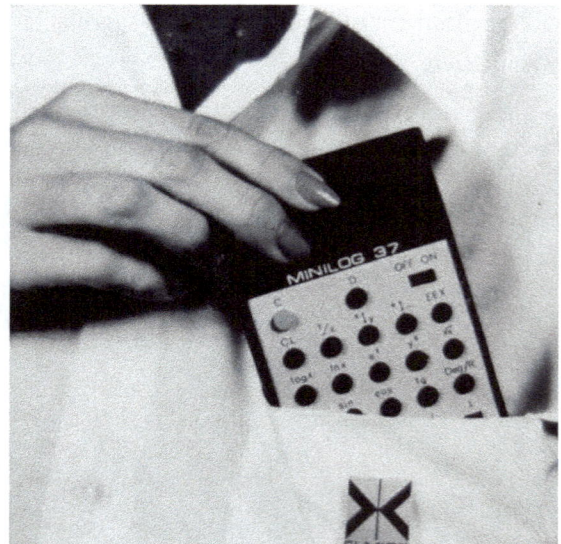

Minilog 37

Chipon 210, electronic calculator, 1971. (Independent project)

"The Chipon 210 model is presented in texts and design reviews as mine and TRS, but it was never TRS's, TRS's electronic engineers were responsible for that. It was a big secret at the time. They tried to create a calculator so that TRS does not know and they hired me to do it, but it never came to life. The idea was to make it as cheap as possible without investing in expensive tools. Polyurethane with hard crust was my solution for the housings."

.   Original model, 1971.   Chipon 210   Model made by 3D printing, 2015.

YU-DESIGN, 1972 – 1973

Although Grünwald never operated under the auspices of the Center for Industrial Design, CIO (indeed, he performed independently in those early years as a kind of competition to the CIO), he was well aware of the importance of organized professional action. Practically parallel to the beginning of his professional work, with fellow designers Vladimir Žitković and Antun Karavanić, he initiated the establishment of the Industrial Design Section at ULUPUH (which first performed together in 1970), and a few years later he was among the initiators of an ambitious project to evaluate the quality of industrial design at the Zagreb fair – YU-DESIGN events. In accordance with his "practical" orientation, the activity organizers linked the quality assessment of the notified products with precisely defined categories, numbered in the questionnaire shared by manufacturers. Among the thirty categories, they were evaluated for general impression, art, ergonomics, economy of material use, transport, technical functions, production technologies, etc. YU-DESIGN was conceived primarily as an ambitious educational action, which should have given manufacturers the benefits of using design. According to YU-DESIGN 72/73, three times in two years the action was carried out and the YU-DESIGN quality label was awarded for 49 products, including Grünwald's machine tools. Unfortunately, the action shut down after a few years, parallel to Grünwald's departure to Canada.

Marko Golub and Koraljka Vlajo

"The situation in all dimensions of industrial design is far from satisfactory and as far as we know, it is not promising. In order to initiate one part of the problem of the large number surrounding this area of human activity, we realized (which is not the first time) that we must engage very actively socially in finding solutions of the problems that are present. The formation of the YU-DESIGN Action Secretariat would take another step forward. As a central task in its program for this moment, the Action Secretary for DESIGN sets the action YU-DESIGN: assessing the quality of industrial design at the events of the Zagreb Fair, both for the past 1972. and the next."

Action Committee, YU-DESIGN 1972/73, 1973.

Design, V. Žitković

"I am sure that some very knowledgable theorists and well informed people about industrial design will declare this system of valorization as a heresy of pure spirit and a violation of the principle of superiority. The YU-DESIGN system does not accept the aristocratic treatment of these problems, but seeks to implement our self-governing socialist society in this undeveloped area with a language that is understandable to every honest and benevolent man. Unlike similar highly regarded prizes where the established criteria of personal knowledge of the entire jury are shared with gold, silver and bronze, which should mark the top, perhaps that's good. YU-DESIGN gives the first time to the manufacturer in writing what its product is in the evaluation of the professional Yugoslav jury, they look through the essential factors in the creation of the product and what has been detailed in detail, such as: general impression, art factor, ergonomics factors, materials economics and transport, technical functions, manufacturing technologies, etc. YU-DESIGN is an action with the basic goal of educating consumers and should be observed and assessed as such"

Antun Karavanić, YU-DESIGN 1972/73, 1973.

Machine tool factory "Prvomajska

It was founded in 1946. It soon became the largest Yugoslav machine tool maker. During the 1980s, the factory employed as many as 7500 workers in plants in Zagreb, Rasa, Ivenec, Golubovac, Donja Stubica, Split, Labin, Drniš and Ozalj. Prvomajska produced primarily machine tools (turning machines, milling, sharpening, sawing of metals, etc.) and machine tools, but production also included hydraulic systems, measuring instruments, petrol station appliances, thermal appliances, gears and reducers for the tractor and car industries, as well as other tools and components. Prvomajska has delivered more than 80 000 machine tools at home and abroad. In the early 1970s Prvomajska collaborated with the designer Davor Grünwald until his departure to Canada, After that machines were designed by Jasenka Mihelčić. Most of the plants after privatization and conversion stopped to exist. Today, only two former plants operate as independent companies: Prvomajska Zagreb and ITAS Prvomajska from Ivanec .

Redesign of mass machine tools for Prvomajska, 1970–1974.

"In Prvomajska I started working on machine tools – automatic sharpener, lathe and others. I immediately noticed that their heavy bases could be made of welded thick sheet metal. They were masters in the cast iron in the sand, but the method of welded sheet metal was far cheaper than casting. All the machines were painted with green Hammerschlag, which for some reason was the European standard. Their sharpener had a conical base, which was visually and physically unstable. I wanted to know why, and the director told me that the engineers demanded that machine look like a silhouette of a man! That didn't make any sense! Installing electronics in such a form was complicated. With my square shape, I have gained walls on which can more easily be placed shelves where the electronics are mounted and far better stability, visually and physically. That was my first request, and they listened to me right away. Aesthetically, I arranged the command panel, according to the ergonomic functions.

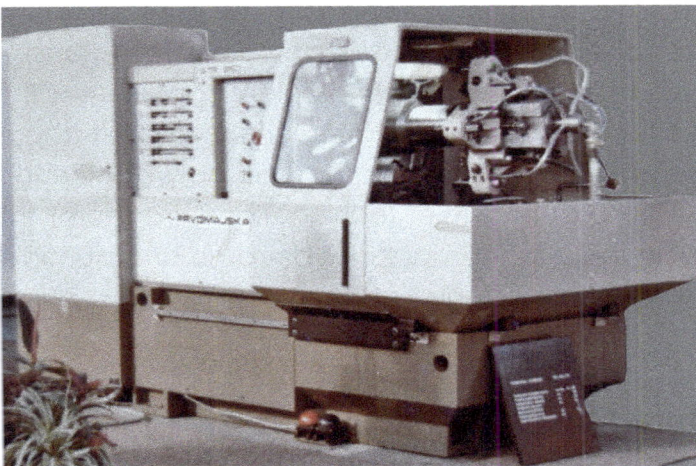

Automatic Lathe

Model 1 : 10

"On the command panel there were all the commands – the elements for visual reading and control (lights) was placed on the upper part, at eye level, while the switches and swivel buttons, for handling, were placed lower, at the height of the bent arm. I put it all visually in order, I suggested a dark brown color for the base and beige for the upper part, which they immediately accepted and thus ultimately changed the color of all their machines."

In 1974, these machines were awarded the City of Zagreb Award and the golden plaque in Leipzig.

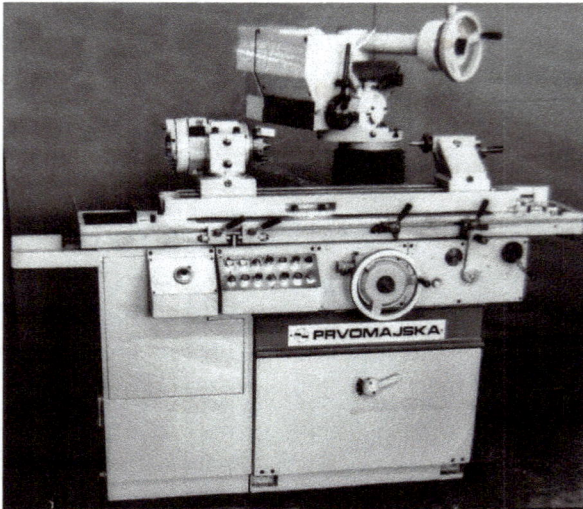

Automatic sharpener

Model 1 : 10

1974. Bernardo Bernardi, on the occasion of the Award of the City of Zagreb to Davor Grünwald: "Although the design of machine tools is a practice almost without any tradition, Davor Grünwald has tackled one of the most complex , and by the material value of the product very responsible for the problem of shaped intervention. By forming a family of machine tools for the Prvomajska factory from Zagreb, he took the only correct path – through a detailed analysis of all those sensitive conditions arising from the human-machine relationship. In this work, Grünwald has demonstrated that he is capable of sensing and combining elements of ergonomic analysis, technical and technological conditions with the complex requirements of high operational functionality. But his intervention doesn't stop at the technical limit. With an exceptional sensibility for artistic phenomena, he was able to turn all the dates of rational instrumentation and the demands of technical and transform into visual reality and harmonious artistic unity. In this way, all machines become an essential element of the overall atmosphere of the working environment."

Metal furniture factory "Jadran"

"Jadran" was founded in 1946. It was named The Metal Furniture Factory and Baby Stroller. In its first years, the baby stroller was its core product, so in 1948. the name of the factory was changed to the

Factory of Baby Strollers. The factory was named "Jadran" in 1953. The production range was complemented by the production of tables and chairs for restaurants and wide-purpose furniture for furnishing schools, offices, theatres and cinemas. In the 1970s, the "Jadran" grew into a leading Yugoslav factory for the production of metal furniture, and in the mid-1980s it employed more than 1,000 workers in four factory plants. The factory is now shut down, but its products such as the Modres, Uni 87 and Ergoline chairs, designed by Mladen Oresić in the 1980s in collaboration with Marijan Orešić, his brother, are still present in many Croatian public spaces from museums to sports halls.

Working chairs for operators with machines, "Jadran", 1972.

Davor Matičević sits on chairs

"These chairs stemmed from talking and observing how operators work alongside the machines that Prvomajska produced. I noticed they were sitting on wooden boxes working with machines. I designed chairs with backrest that had room to move the elbows. The backrest was narrow precisely to allow freedom of movement. The chairs were able to adjust altitude. I ordered prototypes at the "Jadran" factory because no one knew how to process metal pipes so well. At the time, the Director of the "Jadran", Comrade Bujas, offered me the position of director of development, to which I agreed. After three months in the "Jadran", the director invited me to the office and asked me to join the Communist Party since I was in a managerial position. I told him that I had invested heavily in my profession, that I had never been into politics and that I was not interested in politics. So I left the "Jadran". After that, I continued to work in a freelance capacity."

Electronic scale, TTM, 1974.

"I walked into the scale and waiving machine Factory in 1972. Just around the time, engineers were thinking about a new digital scale and we set up a business arrangement.

They gave me the mechanical and electronic components, they were going to use. I took a walk around the stores and analyzed the conditions in which this scale would be used. I concluded that the digital "head" must be turn able to meet the user's ergonomic. I created a through size model and then waited for an answer – what next? At the time, the decision to go to Canada fell through. I left this project and TRS in the legacy of Marijan Orešić, but Marijan never told me what happened to it. The factory ceased operations in the 1990s.

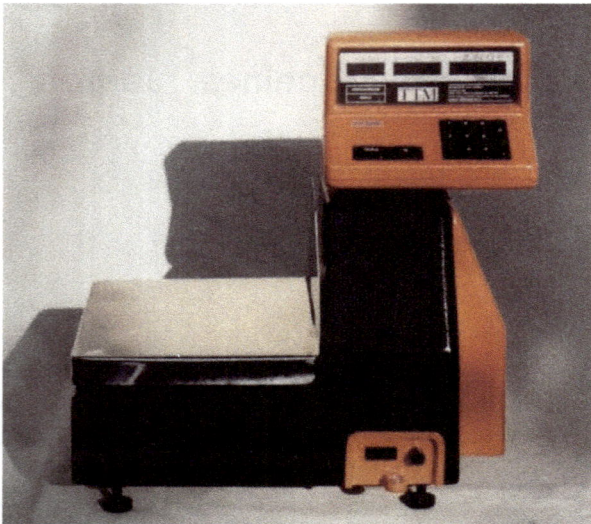

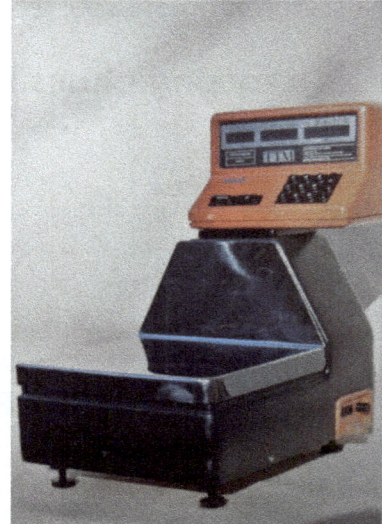

Electronic scale, TTM, 1974.

MICOM – PRODESIGN – VERSITAL

Like Grünwald's arrival from Vienna, and his departure from Yugoslavia – due to the inability to develop an independent professional career – was observed in professional circles, and his later Canadian career was periodically presented in professional magazines such as Industrial Design and the Life of Art. Grünwald's first Canadian years came in search of a "place under the sun" and a rebuilding of a design career. In four years, Grünwald will change several cities (Montreal, Winnipeg, Toronto) and collaborate on a very diverse project – from the design of the household items, computer (Micom 2000), kitchen utensils, and pop-up booths (for consulting company Prodesign) to the redesign of tractors for Versatile. Finally, 1980. Grünwald settled in Toronto, where he got a job as a draftsman at Scintrex, which was involved in the production of geophysical instruments.
 Marko Golub and Koraljka Vlajo

The computer design Micom 2000, 1976.

"On arrival in Canada, I took a job at a company in Montreal that made metal housings for electronics. One of the clients needed computer housing, and a design for that product. The client recognized that he needed my help. He made it necessary to use vacuumed plastic for external skin because it was too risky to invest in expensive steel tools for the injection plastic. That's how this first Canadian computer came into being. It was also my first design in Canada.

Micom 2000

Philips later bought out the project to take a potential competitor off the market. The housing contained all electronics, transformers, a big screen, etc. It was an interesting project, but again one of the collaboration that ended so I couldn't get on with the work anymore. At the beginning of my Canadian career, employers often tried to use me for a small fee because I was a new immigrant."

Pop-up stand and cooking utensils, Prodesign, 1977.

"In Montreal I was briefly employed by the consulting firm Prodesign – it had the same name as my Zagreb office. The owner of this Prodesign was French. For him, I designed a modular and a folding display system. It was a pop-up stand that could be stacked in a box. The concept was very advanced at the time. For the same company, I also designed cooking utensils. It was formally interesting, calm, functional, made of inox with injected plastic, which followed the shape at the holding portion.'

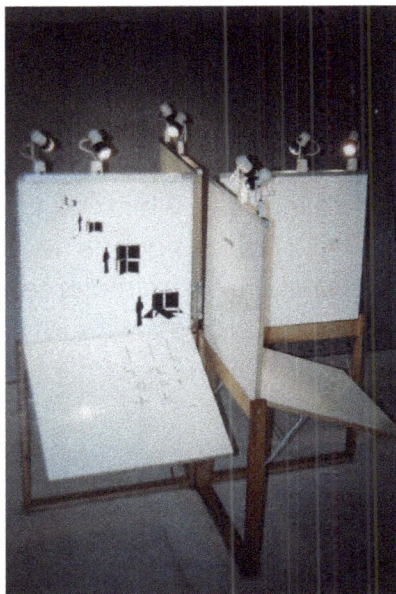

Versital tractor redesign, 1978.

"In Winnipeg, I found a job in the well-established consulting office of the American designer John Vanderhof. With Versital we have arranged to redesign the tractor on the basis of the existing train tract. We had to design a new cabin, control elements as well as all the outer parts of the surface area. Another young industrial designer participated in the project. We agreed that each of us would develop our own tractor concept. The CEO of the tractor factory has carefully analyzed each solution. In the end, he pointed to my drawings and said, "We're going to develop this further because it has a European look and that's what interests us." Versitals' Director liked the European approach in my design, because they intended to offer these tractors on the European market. It's interesting that I wasn't even aware that I was designing "European." My boss was not satisfied, but he had to comply with the decision of the president of Versatile Company."

Versital tractor redesign

Geophysical Industry in Canada

It is known that Toronto is a world center for the geophysical industry. All the strong geophysical companies are located in Toronto. This Canadian industry has evolved from the need to extract Canadian wealth in ores and minerals. Davor Grünwald got by chance a job at Scintrex and later at Geonics, Sensors & Software and Gem Systems. He practically had a monopoly as an industrial designer in that industry, which he trough his work has educated. He gave a gift to Canada as an industrial designer – he ennobled a strong Canadian geophysical industry with aesthetic and ergonomic elements. No new Canadian geophysical device goes through the development process without design intervention thanks to Grünwald's long-running work.
Marko Golub and Koraljka Vlajo

SCINTREX

Scintrex was founded in 1946. under the name Sharpe Instruments Ltd. This Canadian company specializes in the production of mechanical magnetometers, electrical measuring instruments and electromagnetic systems for mineral and ore exploration systems.

After the company bought Seigel Associates Ltd. in 1967. they change the name to Scintrex. During the 1970s and 1980s, Scintrex developed new technologies and production programs (spectrometers, Luminex system) and expanded its production of seismological research and geophysical measurements. In the early 1980s, Scintrex decided to step up in improving the quality of its products and hired Davor Grünwald to develop the design of the electromagnetic receiver and transmitter Genie, which was launched in 1982., which was awarded with the Canada Design Award. Scintrex also operates today, primarily in the field of development and production of gravimeters, magnetometers and other geophysical instruments.

Atomic absorption spectrophotometer AAZ-2, Scintrex, 1980.

"Through head-hunter, I got a job as a draftsman at Scintrex (Scientific Instruments, Research and Exploration), a company that also manufactures geophysical devices. I didn't work as an industrial designer at first; I walked through the "small door" as a draftsman. The draftsman's would sit at their desks and the boss would sit in front and supervise.

D. Grünwald, "operator"

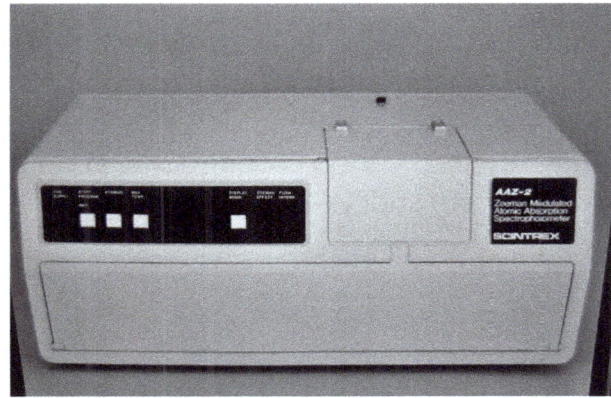

Everyone was getting their own project and had "free hands" to design as they feel like. However, I did it my way – I would make a drawing and immediately start making the model. The boss was wondering at it, and I was explaining to him that I was exploring what I was doing and would like to see in three dimensions. I didn't want to know who I have been yet. I designed an interesting, complicated instrument (AAZ-2), a sample of the solution was placed in the instrument, and the instrument would analyze particles of gold or silver. It was interesting because I could organize an ergonomic approach, visual appearance, an easy way to put samples and access electronics."

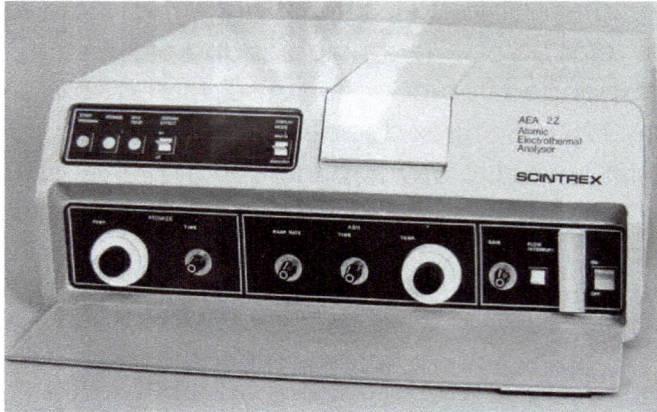

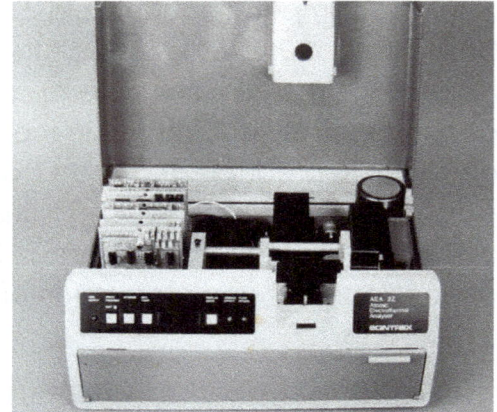

Cardboard model

The electromagnetic transmitter and receiver SE-88, Genie, 1982,

"Geophysical "backpack" instrument Genie was designed in 1982 and was intended to search for metal objects at a depth of up to 10 meters. According to my information, this was the first geophysical device in North America, and perhaps in the world, treated with industrial design. I designed that device for Scintrex after I left them. Here's a brief description of these circumstances: President invited me to an interview because he noticed that I was "Something else." I gave him a lecture on industrial design and the role of designers in a development/production corporation. I asked him if he'd be willing to put me in that function with a bigger salary. He answered briefly NO! The next day I left Scintrex. They came after me and signed a contract to develop the design of the Genie System for a far higher fee than my salary."

Genie transmitter and receiver

"Genie has the characteristics of exceptional ergonomics, an integrated battery pack for rapid exchange and rational production technology for small batches. That system won the Canada Design Award in 1982. I was especially pleased because that was my "revenge" for their treatment while I was employed by them." "Genie consists of a transmitter and receiver. The transmitter was placed on the operator's back with an integrated battery pack that could be replaced quickly. The receiver was worn on the chest – ergonomically quite a demanding problem."

  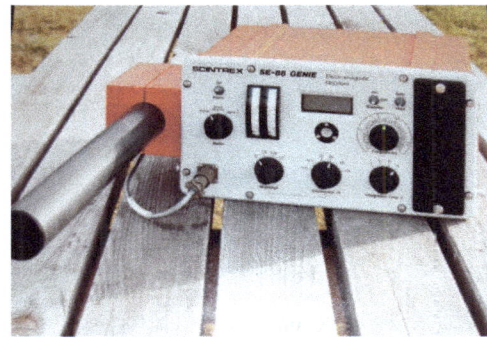

Transmitter   Receiver

"Genie was used for research under the surface of the earth. The operators were standing about 20 meters away from each other. The transmitter sends magnetic field passing through the earth and if they encounter conductive material, they react and a deviation of the magnetic field will be registered in the receiver and then in the compute. That determines the position (GPS) and how deep "something" is located. For Genie housing I used solid polyurethane with a heavy skin. t's a relatively cheap technology and molds can be made of wood. In doing so, I avoided very expensive aluminum or steel molds for injection plastic. The geophysical industry doesn't have a high production – if they made and sell a hundred of these systems a year, that's a lot. For these reasons, geophysical devices are very expensive."

DELPHAX SYSTEMS

Denison Corporation and the Canadian Development Corporation (CDC) founded De phax Systems in 1980. With the aim of exploring the possibilities for the advancement of photocopying technology. Delphax System engineers are responsible for developing revolutionary fast printing technology (ion deposition), and based on this technology Delphax soon developed new fast printers whose design is signed by Davor Grünwald. In 1984, the CDC announced that In 1997, they sold their shares to a competing company, 1997. The American Xerox fully purchased Delphax Systems.

"After leaving Scintrex, I found an ad in the paper that Delphax was looking for an industrial designer. I immediately answered and went to an interview and got a job for twice as much salary as in Scintrex. After close studies of the circumstances in which such a printer will be working , I have made 3D renders, sketched the principles on which these machines work, studied ergonomics and technological conditionality's, made models, and solved graphic tasks. I presented it all to fellow engineers and thereby gave them indications of the directions of development of these products."

Delphax Corporate Identity, 1983.

"I also devised a new corporate identity for them, a trademark and a logo, because their original was not readable. On one occasion, the Japanese delegation came and they couldn't read it. The president then asked me to create a new trademark and logo. I also devised the concept of an exhibition stand from Alucobond. It is an interesting and "sandwich" material, which is used for the tilling of houses. Between the two thin aluminum sheet is a semi-solid spongy material (foam core), all together 8 millimeters thick.

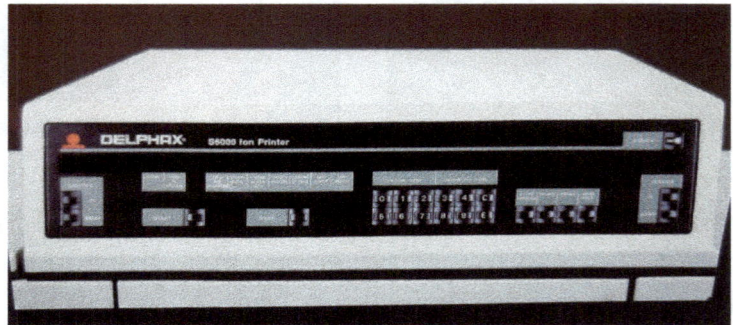

Front panel of the printer with logo

Davor Grünwald is the designer of modernism, an era of absolute faith in the possibility that through social and technological innovations can solve all the world's woes, the beliefs of the designers at the time that industrialization, standardization and mass production (with their help) will bring happiness and prosperity to the entire community. Practitioner with knowledge of electrical engineering, Grünwald primarily solves the problem, both the client (the manufacturer) and the user satisfaction. The product will be improved with the help of functional and constructive procedures (reducing the consumption of materials, simplifying the production process), while always acting as a lawyer for the future user.

Marko Golub and Koraljka Vlajo

Exhibition stand, Delphax (Davor pictured)

Fast ion printers - Delphax, 1981. – 1984.

I was admitted to Delphax in 1981. Engineers have already worked on the concept of a "printing engine". At this stage, I could suggest to the development team ergonomiclly justified positions of functional handles and approaches to change the toner and "printing cartridges"(the main part of the technology where negative ions are formed in the form of the printable ions).

Engine & Sketches related to the development of ion printing, printing machine, image formation

The first printers were with a vertical paper shift, the design of Delphax engineers. The engineers insisted on that because such a printer took up a small floor space. These printers were intended for conferences where huge amounts of material were to be printed quickly to participants. I quickly realized that this "vertical" version was ergonomically not correct"

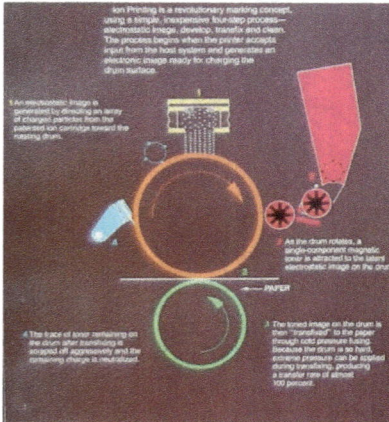

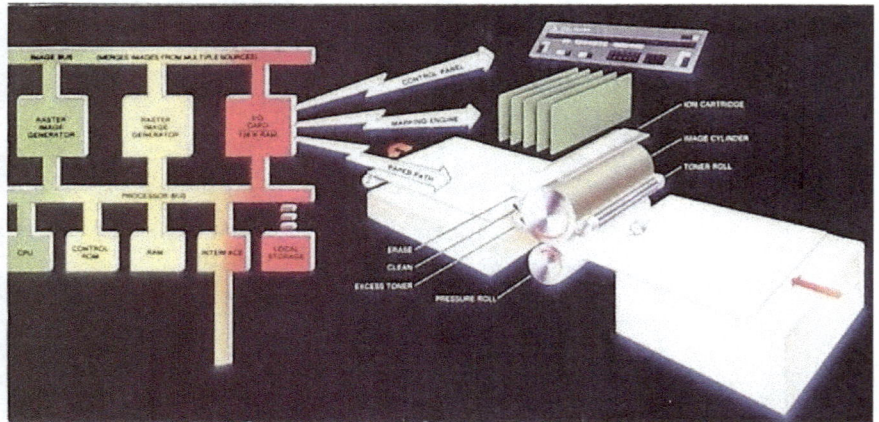

Graphic representation of the principles of ion printing, D. Grünwald

I began to propagate the concept of horizontal paper displacement, so that the paper input and output were at the same height. It took me a long time to convince the managers. I convinced them by, without their knowledge, I made a model in the right size in my garage. I borrowed the printer components from the company.

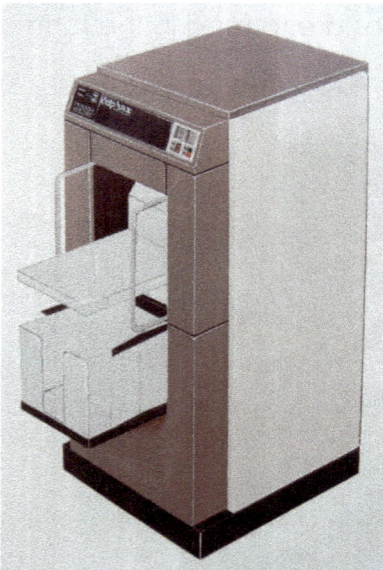

Sketch, "vertical" Ion Printer   Prototype, "vertical" Ion Printer   Model, 1:10, "horizontal" I Ion Printer

One weekend, I took my model to the president's office and left it there. On Monday morning I waited for his reaction and heard his shout of surprise. He asked who did it? I came up to him and explained to him that it was my presentation for him, which I did at home, because no one at Delphax listened to me.   And so began my real industrial designer function in that company. The president of the company gave me all the powers I and suddenly I found myself in a position to lead engineers according to the concept I created. That was before Xerox and IBM and their horizontal printers.

One weekend, I took my model to the president's office and left it there. On Monday morning I waited for his reaction and heard his shout of surprise. He asked who did it? I came up to him and explained to him that it was my presentation for him, which I did at home, because no one at Delphax listened to me.   And so began my real industrial designer function in that company. The president of the company gave me all the powers I and suddenly I found myself in a position to lead engineers according to the concept I created. That was before Xerox and IBM and their horizontal printers.

Model of "horizontal" ion printer made in my garage

Model "Horizontal" printer

I often did sophisticated 3D presentations in color, at a time when it could not yet be done with the help of a computer. The president asked me to make about two dozen small models in a ratio of 1 to 10, in order to give them to potential clients.

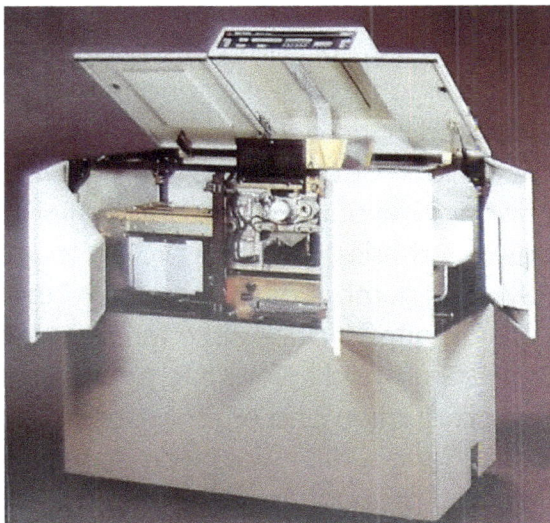

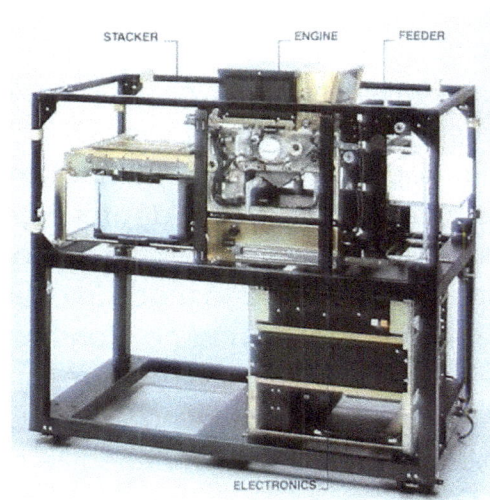
"Horizontal" ion printer, produced, open view

I suggested to the company's management that they use the "vertical" concept for classic office printers, where it is not necessary to print such large quantities of documents as at conferences. It is important that the floor space that occupies the printer is as small as possible. They accepted my proposal."

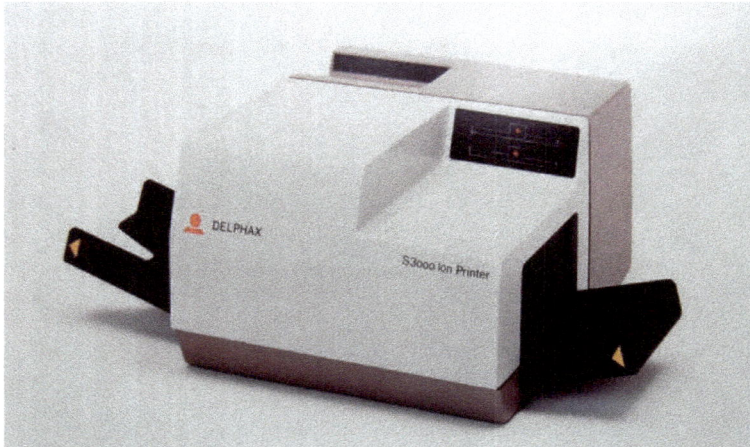

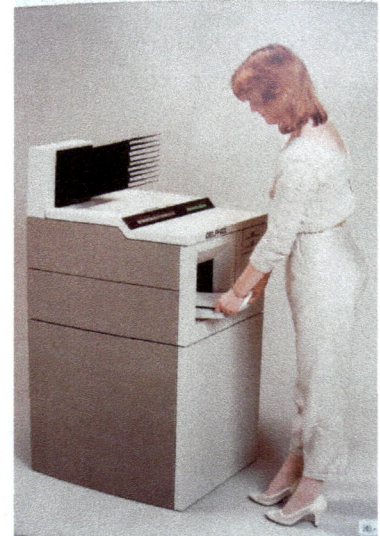

Office. "vertical" ion printer

"Delphax's marketing vice president (I later learned he was a CIA intelligence officer) kicked me out of the company because I made a new trademark in red and it was supposed to be blue - a traditional American color. I got a lot of monetary damages because he threw me out for no valid reason (wrongful dismissal) and he was kicked out of Delphax right behind it.'

GEONICS LTD

Geonics Ltd founded in 1962. and it was based in Toronto, Canada, and for the first years Geonics was primarily involved in equipment applicable for surface natural resource research. In the mid-1970s, the Geonics specialized in the development of equipment for electromagnetic research methods. Instruments such as EM31, EM34-3, EM38, EM61 for the exploration of different soil depths have significantly expanded the application of Geonics products – from agriculture and archaeology to forensics. Geonics products are extremely complex, expensive and made in a relatively small number of specimens. At the same time, they require careful handling, transfer and use on often inaccessible terrain. The company therefore in the mid-1980s hired designer Davor Grünwald to improve product design: from technological solutions in the systemization of production and ergonomics of use to the aesthetics of the design of the entire production range. Grünwald worked with the Geonics until 2008. Geonics is still one of the world's leading producer's of electromagnetic geophysical equipment.

Conductivity meter EM38, Geonics,

1985. "After I lost my job in Delphax, I happened to meet a colleague I ran with as an athlete at the Mladost club next to Sava river in Zagreb. I told him what I do for a living. He invited me to come to the company for an interview because he has a problem with one product. That product looked like a wooden board with electronics and antennas scattered around. They wanted it to be made "nicer." I applied a concept where all the electronics are attached to the front display and via the connector connected to the antennas and the battery. The handle is integrated into the cherry frame in the balance position of the device. The distance between the transmitter and the receiving antenna is exactly one meter, small deviations are corrected electronically. Cherry wood is the most stable of all non-metallic materials – the coefficient of tightening/stretching is the smallest of all. The cherry frame is processed with a CNC milling machine. This instrument has become an inevitable, standard device in agronomy when examining the quality of the soil, but also in archaeology when searching for "cavities" in the soil, as well as in police activities, to search for fresh graves. About a hundred pieces are produced a year and cost like a small Hyundai car. "

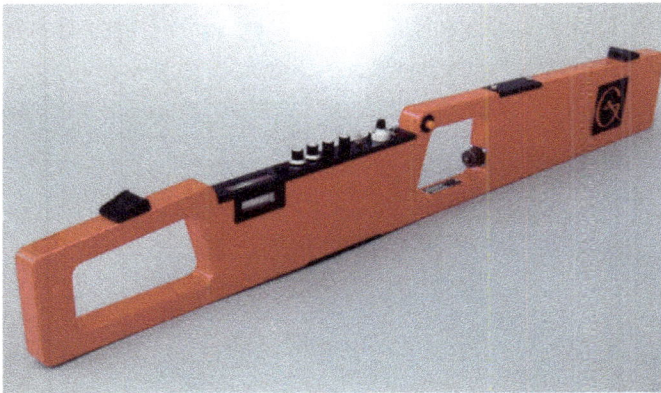

EM38, geophysical instrument

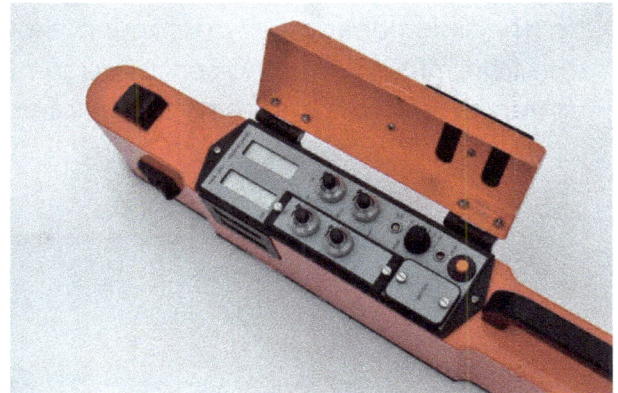

"Double" version

Encapsulated geophysical antenna, Geonics, 1986.

"It's a small series again, so I had to use cheap technology. It is made of vacuum plastic (ABS) – one mold was used for the lower and upper half, which represents savings. When installed antenna together with electronics, the space is being filled with semi-hard polyurethane to protect against moisture. The color is red again, which is noticeable in the bush."

Encapsulated geophysical antenna, Geonics, 1986.

EM39, Winch for lowering Geophysical Probes, Geonics, 1990.

"The EM39 winch was a fairly complicated mechanical device containing an electric motor, a cable drum, a cable winding system and an electronic device at the top. It's a geophysical device that lowers the probe into a hole about two kilometers deep and is used to check for leakage of contaminated water. The principle is the same as with other devices, the transmitting antenna sends magnetic field into the space around and the receiving antenna receives and records deviations due to the penetration of contaminated water."

EM39, Winch. 1990.

EM61 – Geophysical instrument for finding buried with toxic waste, Geonics, 1989 – 2000

EM61, Electromagnetic System

Control Device (right)

'It's about two powerful (heavy) antennas and batteries on wheels. It's easier to drive that load on wheels than to carry. The transmitter antenna produces a magnetic field up to 100 meters deep. The principle of how these electromagnetic devices work: the transmitter sends magnetic field through the earth. The receiver receives these magnetic field that if they encounter a conductive medium, the computer analyzes this data and determines where the location (GPS) is in what size and at what depth "something" is located. A great device for finding buried barrels with toxic waste. Before I got to the Geonics, the antennas were made with polyester. The water was entering through the tiny pores and had to be thrown away after a short use. I changed the technology and used semi-hard polyurethane. These problems didn't happen again.

For several Geonics electromagnetic systems, I developed a control, electronic device (2000) where I applied injection plastic for the housing (Photo right). In fact, I proved to my superior that it's smarter to put $12,000 in an aluminum tool for injection plastic than to fabricate a $100 electronics box each time. A box of injection plastic costs $8! In 10 years, the Geonics has saved $100,000. The top and bottom cover are identical – it only takes one tool. The concept of this device is in principle identical to the concept of TRS's battery calculator – the electronics are calibrated (tuned) without lids, which I invented in 1972. in Zagreb. The Geonics' advantage over the competition is its square and round antennas, technologically made according to my instructions, they are hard to copy. Ronald Regan ordered the cleansing of America from discarded and buried, in metal barrels, toxic waste. Then Geonics sold a large quantity of EM61 and so overtopped the competition.

Protem geophysical instrument, 2001.

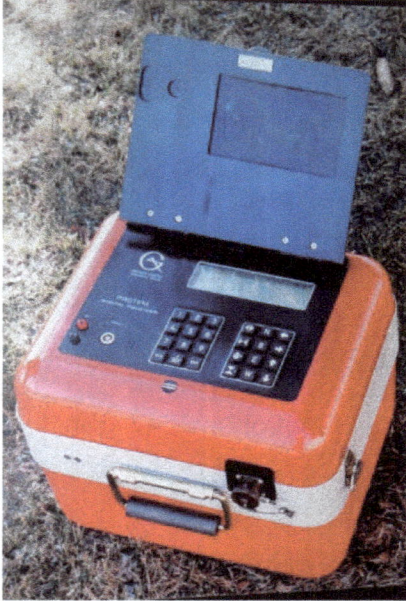

Protem

Strong EM61 (example of very complicated device)

I made sure that the front panel of the instrument made logical sense, to make it all clear. The box was purchased; it's a typical approach to design in the geophysical industry. The trick is how to place all the electronics in a box that was purchased from the shelf"

Landmine and Metal Objects Finder, Geonics, 2002.

That year I worked on such a device, which can be used in two ways: if you are looking for landmines, then it is used without wheels and to search for metal objects, with wheels. The word is about a very interesting product because I had to integrate the transmitter and reception antenna into one assembly. I developed a whole new technological method to achieve what I wanted. I've had wheels from previous systems. I used an electronic control device from an EM61 device and it was mounted on a carry stick."

Landmine and metal objects detection device

*

By the time he retired in 2008., Grünwald has designed a number of extremely complex products for the Geonics, which incorporate an almost non-existent ergonomic component. These are instruments that require intense interaction with the user: they are portable, folding, require precise handling and reading of data. It is precisely in such tasks that Grünwald's talent comes to the forefront.

Marko Golub and Koraljka Vlajo

SENSORS & SOFTWARE

Sensors & Software is a Canadian company founded in 1988. year. The company was created with the aim of commercializing the new GPR (ground penetrating radar) technology, pulse EKKO, initially intended solely for application in geophysical research. However, this technology soon found its application in a variety of disciplines and areas – from concrete scanning, forensics and ice thickness measurements to Search & Rescue operations. In the mid-1990s, the company hired Davor Grünwald to design the portable digital underground radar PulseEKKO 100.

PulseEKKO 100 digital underground radar, Sensors & Software, 1994.

"It's an instrument to control cast concrete, if there are cracks. It can determine the thickness of the ice and look for gold or silver. The concept was based on one-handed conduct, rapid battery exchange and clean front panel graphics. The housing was conditioned by the owner of the company, black anodized aluminum. Later, they applied the bright yellow that I suggested in a first place (visible in the bushes). I fixed the PC motherboard to the front panel and it is connected to other electrical components via the connector. When I started working on this project, the electronic

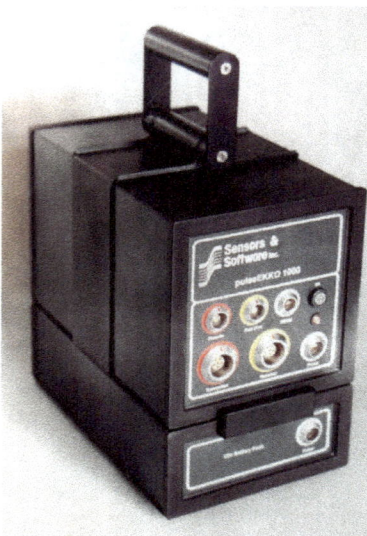

Ekko radar system, Sensors & Software, 1994.

engineers had electrical components assembled, but scattered around the table. They hired me just in time. I was also this time the organizer of these components but under the influence, as always, ergonomic and productive - technological conditions. In this type of instrument, I pay great attention to the front panel graphics. In this case it worked very well."

It can be said that Grünwald's experience in the geophysical industry briefly recapitulates his design path: from stubborn insistence on thoughtful design treatment and insistence on ergonomic characteristics of products of trying to incorporate institutional support in the field of industrial design that, during the reign of mass production, did not attract the attention of professional associations. With this fanaticism, he achieved   professional respect in an inert industry that surrendered to design quite reluctantly and only after long-term assurances about the comparative advantages of industrial design investment.

Marko Golub and Koraljka Vlajo

GEM SYSTEMS

GEM has a long history. They started as a consulting company for geophysical and electromagnetic systems. The company incorporated itself in 1980 as GEM Systems and is now known worldwide by that name. GEM Systems was founded by Dr. Ivan Hrvoić and Dr. Jasna Hrvoić. The company is run by Dr. Ivan Hrvoić, who brings many years of experience in geophysical instruments and electronics design. Dr. Hrvoić has developed famous magnetometer and gradiometer technologies. GEM Systems is the world's leading company in these technologies as well as Gem surface solutions (GEM Ground Solutions) as well as Gem flying solutions (GEM Airborne Solutions)

Geophysical Bird, Gem Systems, 2008.

"Gem Systems is run by Ivan Hrvoić, a Toronto-based From Zagreb who worked at Scintrex in the 1960s - which I later worked for. Many years ago, in his garage, he began inventing earth-based geophysical instruments, instruments that don't produce their own magnetic field, but use Earth magnetism. He invented sensors that "feel" these magnetism, and if something is conductive in the soil, they will deform and the computer will indicate what it is. All those sensors I developed (mechanically) for Hrvoić. I had to "pack" very sophisticated laser and optical technology into a plastic cylinder - from an industrial design aspect of a rather uninteresting shape (three sizes: large, medium and small). But it took three years of development! Such sensors are mounted on the "bird", the same design of mine, worn by a helicopter. The computer in the helicopter registers the data and the teams on the ground go to the designated locations and are still investigating but now with more details. I worked for him for 20 years on a contract basis. He often goes to Croatia and invests in geophysics at the Zagreb University. He's one of the leading authorities in the world in this field.

Geophysical "bird"

CONCEPTS / UNREALIZED WORKS

Oxygen production machine, sketches, 1990.

"In the case of an oxygen machine, the concept is based on the fact that from lead rods exposed to peroxide, pure oxygen and drinking water are obtained." I earned a few patents in that project. In the case of an accident in the mine, the air is gone; the machine produces oxygen and water, two basic components for survival in these conditions. I am particularly sorry that there has not been a realization of this technology in the application in the mines. Canada financially supported the project, but it did not materialize because the client had no money for the production. These days, I've noticed that oxygen production technology for personal use has gone further."

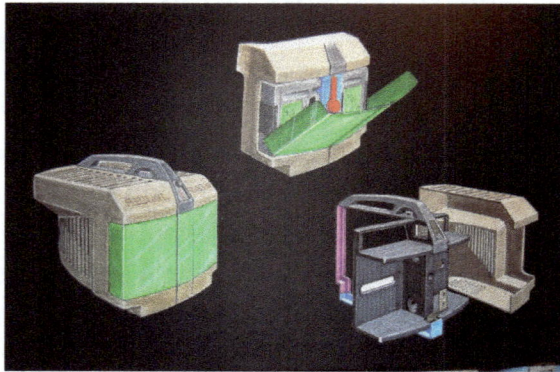

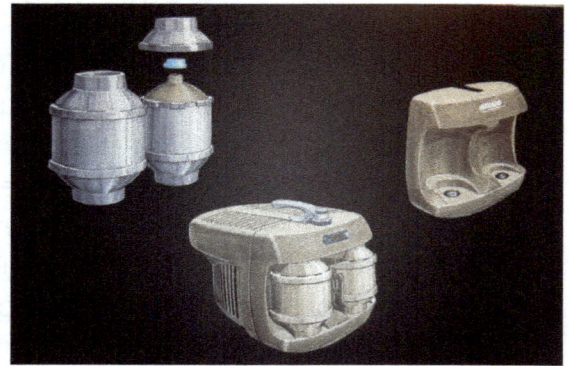

Disassembled wine/oil barrel, sketches, 2003.

Disassembled wine/oil barrel, sketches, 2003.

My wine and oil barrel is based on the 30-year-old concept of putting these in inert four-layer plastic bags. When pouring out, the air does not enter the bags, so the wine or oil does not get spoiled. It is planned that the barrels should be applied in wineries where they often pour their wine when tasting. The bag is held by a polypropylene barrel composed of parts produced from rotomolding technology. The project was not realized because of the costly tools."

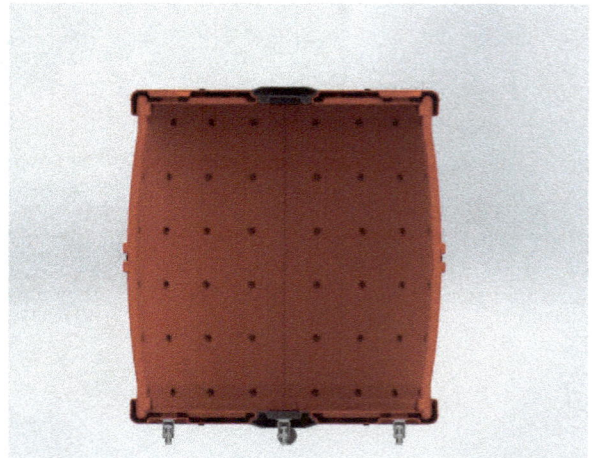

SELF-INITIATED WORKS SINCE 2008. UNTIL TODAY

Although, since 2008, Grünwald is retired, he understood his profession as a mission rather than a job, did not give up design. He works on smaller projects that he can produce in his own production and which stem mainly from his needs or opportunities he has noticed in his immediate surroundings: car trunk, bicycle accessory, armchair, chair. These projects, without an industrial bag round, are characterized by charming simplicity, a concise, ascetic DIY approach based on the search for the fastest and most economical intelligent solution as if their author, rather than at the end of a professional path, had found himself again at the very beginning where he sought to rediscover his understanding of the design. And that's when it's stripped to the very core, it's actually very simple. In fact, during the preparations for this exhibition we finally asked him what the design profession meant to him, and he just reminded us of the passion he felt seeing that mentioned exhibition of Italian design at the Zagreb Museum of Arts and Crafts in 1963. That's what I want to do, that's me.
Marko Golub and Koraljka Vlajo

Rack for Porsche Boxster, 2011.

When I retired. I rewarded myself with that beauty, I always wanted it. I secretly saved up from the fees I earned on the side. I ran into that car, it was two years old and bought it at half price. With my wife we go on excursions and often run into cheap fruit in baskets or antique furniture. When we go on holiday, a large plastic suitcase is attached to the trunk. I designed the trunk for that purpose. That car has space for things at the front and the rear side because the engine is in the middle, but still does not have enough room. So I made the rack for my own purposes – two aluminum plates were cut with the help of a water jet, which works by cutting thick material under the intense pressure of water in which there is small sand.

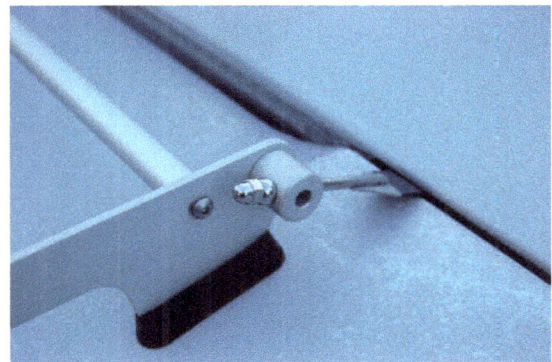

Amazing technology! These plates are connected by aluminum tubes. So assembled trunk is mounted on the rear trunk lid with stainless steel buckles coated with plastic so that the edges of the lid are not damaged. Porsche doesn't offer its trunk rack. I offered them my design, but they turned me down because they generally don't collaborate with outside designers. But so far I have sold a dozen racks to my "colleagues". I order all the pieces, so when the order arrives; I put it in a disassembled form in a relatively small box and send it. I'm having fun, as pensioner!"

Chair Ellips, 2015.

Chair Elips, laminated wood, painted

'In retirement I started dealing with things that interested me, but I didn't have time for them before. So began work on the chair Ellipse. I simply gave myself the task: in the world, there are a "small million" different chairs, I was wondering if I could design one for which I did not need expensive tools, to use painted, laminated wood (ply) or hardwood, that there are no screws and welding. I've been having fun with it for three years and the result is, harmoniously, aesthetically beautiful, ergonomically correct chair. I called it the Elips because I found that this form satisfies the seating area and the backrest. I protected the design in Europe. An interesting detail is the attaching of the leg (stainless steel rod of 12 mm diameter) in wood. The rod is profiled so that when it is glued with epoxy, that detail is very solid. I fell twice (the chair collapsed) until I found a solution. The legs at the end have plasticized balls so that the chair does not glide on a smooth surface. That detail is also on the backrest for hanging bags. The curve of the backrest is good for hanging coat. One of my colleagues, the designer, called that chair Ant."

"I decided to fabricate ellipse chairs in my arrangement and give them to the people who helped me out."

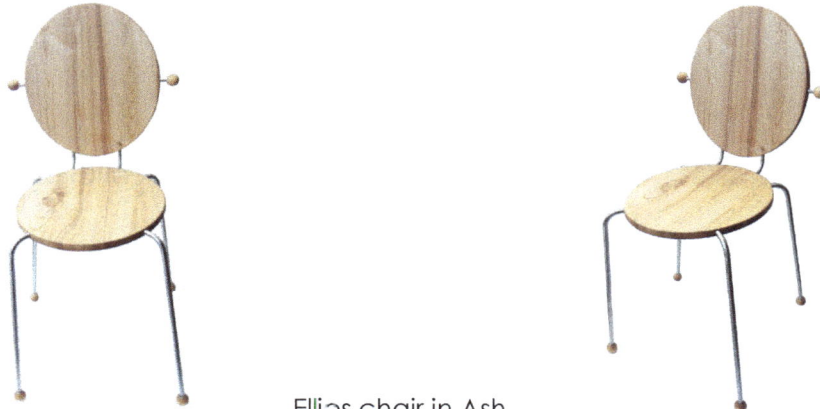

Ellios chair in Ash

Bike safety stick, 2016.   Saves lives!

A 76cm long, 3.6cm diameter rod of semi-hard polyurethane sponge is attaches under the seat and directed to the left side (in England on the right). It is red/orange in color (florescent). Cars that overtake a bicycle are "forced" to circumvent the bicycle in a wide arc. When storing the bike, the rod is turned parallel to the bike. The parts are as follows: Purchasing clamp, polyurethane rod glued to the rod holder. The safety rod can be mounted to any bicycle in minutes.

Bike safety stick pictures

Historically significant trademarks of Davor Grünwald

Trademark Prodesign, consulting studio, 1969. Within the ideal form (circle) compromises of influential elements.

TRS trademark 1970. Inspired by the rudimentary binary method with which TRS engineers began experimenting before electronic calculator operations.

Delphax trademark 1983. symbolizing, the particle of the toner imprints on paper

Trademark of Consulting Study of Croatian/Canadian Industrial/Product designer Davor Grünwald, 2016.   INVENTIVE PRODUCT DESIGN (IPD)

Patricia Počanić emblem, 2020.

Creative/thought process when creating a trademark, the emblem is very similar to the creation of a three-dimensional object. That's why I was happy to get into these graphic creations.

*

Interesting questions and answers from a series of conversations (6) with Mrs. Jasna Lovrinčević

Jasna Lovrinčević: How do you feel, surrounded by all your works, placed in one place at the Technical Museum Nikola Tesla in Zagreb?

Davor Grünwald: This is the first time I've been exposed to everything in one place. I was asking myself, so did I really do these all in 50 years? At the opening I heard often: Well done! The visitors were really intrigued by what they saw. Excellent, intelligent texts from curators Koraljka Vlajo and Marko Golub certainly contributed to this. Graphic designer Barbara Blasin has set up the exhibit – top notch!

Jasna Lovrinčević: In your memoirs you describe your visit to the exhibition of Italian design in Zagreb, 1963. When you said to yourself, **"Well, that's me**!" In this exhibition you can rightly say, "That's me." Do you still feel this delightful with industrial design?

Davor Grünwald: That phrase of mine "That's me" has now become my emblem. It appears in texts and interviews. Of course, when this exhibition opened, in my speech I mentioned it, but now I look back, unlike that time in 1963. when I just felt a strong intuitive urge. I can only describe that moment; It was like I was struck by lightning, and that's when I went energetically, but secretly, to become an industrial designer. This enthusiasm and sense of fulfillment persist today, but in these retirement years, as an intense hobby.

Jasna Lovrinčević: Due to your enthusiasm for industrial design, you have stopped studying the Electrical Engineering in Zagreb and you have done everything to enter industrial design. Convinced of what you wish, you travelled to Vienna, passed the demanding entrance exam and thus, together with four other candidates out of thirty who took the exam, gained the right to enroll in the Academy of Applied Arts in Vienna (Akademie für Angewandte Kunst, Wien). After completing your studies, fruitful, creative work in Croatia as well as in Canada followed, accompanied by numerous accolades and awards, but also difficulties, mainly due to political circumstances. Is there an industrial design area that you might have wanted to work on and you didn't have the chance?

Davor Grünwald: You've done a good job of showing me in short lines my journey. No one's asked me that before. I have done every project very intensively and have been happy and satisfied that I have an object on which I can profess to the extreme "content". For these reasons, I have never aspired to any group of specific products. Diversity filled me completely, so this is what this exhibition notes: from kitchen utensils, to tractors to Porsche trunks.

Jasna Lovrinčević: This exhibition aims to emphasize that your work is related to technology and is also entitled: "Industrial design in the context of technology". However, your Sculptra, created as a mathematical solution to one student theoretical task in the second semester of your study in 1964. comes out of this context and has primarily one prominent aesthetic aspect. The contrast of light and shadow on its rounded surfaces captures the view of visitors and their interest in this exceptional design. Sculptra is actually a form of materials and practical application. Can designs even be imagined without an aesthetic component?

Davor Grünwald: The answer is short: Can't ! Proportions, colors, materials, ergonomics – this makes the design of the product. The balance of these components is in a compromise relationship, determines the characteristics in technological-production terms. The Eastern philosophy of yin and yang says that the condition of surviving everything in the micro and macro world is a balance. I applied this philosophy to my approach to industrial design and as far back as 1968. year. That's what I displayed with the trademark of my consulting office, Prodesign. The perfect form of the circle contains within itself compromises of influencing factors.

Jasna Lovrinčević: The modern world is unimaginable without design. Can you imagine your life without design?

Davor Grünwald: Certainly, NO ! Well-formed objects affect our moods; color, shape, harmony, functionality. With maximum safe handling, we gain "trust" towards the subject. Because of the good design, our life is easier, more sophisticated, and more comfortable. I've always maintained that I have a strong intuition and that I follow that feeling religiously. My life decisions were largely driven by intuition, and each project required strong intuition. I think "as designer" so I can't imagine a life without a design.

Jasna Lovrinčević: Your whole life you have been successful, your design is equally highly regarded in both Croatia and Canada and has been crowned, in addition to numerous design awards, high recognition, ULUPUH Grand Prize for lifetime achievement. Your latest ELLIPS chair design indicates one inexhaustible inventiveness and openness to new challenges. Can you say a little more about yourself, in terms of what inspires and encourages you, In 2018. in May, you participated in an exhibit in Split together with Boris Ljubicic. From November 2019. to 1. February 2020. at the Nikola Tesla Technical Museum, TMNT, an exhibition was held: Davor Grünwald, industrial design in the context of technology, with texts by curators Marko Golub and Koraljka Vlajo. Barbara Blasin did an excellent job on the graphic design aspect of the exhibit.

Davor Grünwald: My intuition has always served me well. You must have a predisposition, faith in yourself and perseverance. I surround myself with creative, stimulating people. If I want to achieve something, I'm trying to find a few ways to achieve it. Along the way I go through disappointments, failures, dissatisfaction, but I remain unwavering, or stubborn. A positive thread of guiding, by some law of probability, throws me to the surface and I see the light of the day. It's a feeling I aspire to, a sense of accomplishment! The last few years have happened to me, the Lifetime Achievement Award, three exhibitions, a little Monograph and all that stuff with articles and interviews – it greatly encourages me in this retirement age to continue to create and seek creative engagement. I can't forget my colleagues who help me directly or indirectly. You can't do anything on your own! People tell me I'm lucky. I answer; I've never won the lottery before. i build my own happiness.

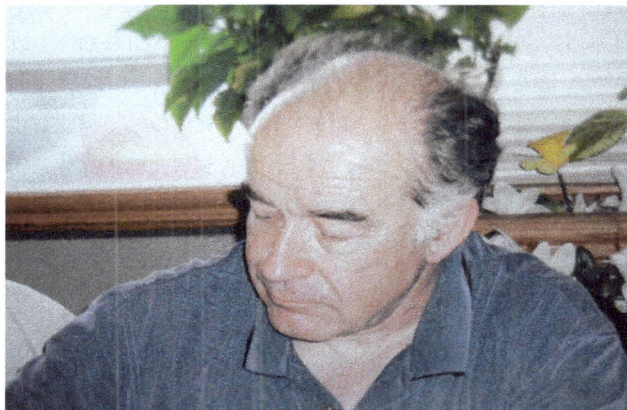

Davor Grünwald, 62

2018. In May, he exhibits in Split together with Boris Ljubičić

2019. From November 2019. to 1. February 2020. at the Nikola Tesla Technical Museum, TMNT, an exhibition was held: **Davor Grünwald, industrial design in the context of technology**, with texts by curators Marko Golub and Koraljka Vlajo. Barbara Blasin did the graphic design.

Markita Franulić, Davor Grünwald, Koraljka Vlajo, Marko Golub, Photo: Palma Orlović

A welcome speech by Davor Grünwald at the opening ceremony of the exhibition at the Nikola Tesla Technical Museum, November 2019.

Good evening, I am immensely pleased to welcome, friends, colleagues and members of my family who have come tonight to this very beautifully presented exhibition. A special thank you goes to Ms. Markita Franulić, director of the Technical Museum, Nikola Tesla, who facilitated the realization of this exhibition.

My half-century of work as an industrial designer in Croatia and Canada is here before you. I remember, it wasn't easy - to constantly prove, reassure and at the same time educate the clients or employers on the value of my approaches in their product development processes. Croatian six-year, very prolific period after graduation, in Canada "opened the door for me" Later, through quality work, I simply imposed myself on that new homeland Canada. Failures and disappointments were present in my path. At the end of the "underlined line" is which is worth. This exhibition confirms that it was worth being stubborn and following instincts, guiding light. Now, my entire professional opus is stored in the Museum of Arts and Crafts (MUO) in Zagreb. This came at the suggestion of a colleague Ljubičić 2015, thank you! And that was the place in 1964. in which I "recognized myself" at the Italian design exhibition, what I wanted to do it. I shouted, "It's me"! The point of this exhibition is that changes in technological terms affect the solutions of industrial designers and Vice Versa design ideas can influence technological change. From this angle I have processed all my projects: it has happened in the past, it happens in the present and it will be present in the future. I would suggest young industrial designers closely monitor the world's technological advances. I especially thank Ms. Koraljka Vlajo, curator of design at the MUO, Mr. Marko Golub, head of HDD gallery, Ms. Barbara Blasin for the graphic design of the exhibition and Ms. Markita Franulić, director of the Technical Museum, Nikola Tesla for their understanding and presentation to the audience of my historical role in the development of industrial / product design. Thank you so much!

Exhibition at the Nikola Tesla Technical Museum in Zagreb:

Davor Grünwald, industrial design in the context of technology, November 2019. - January 2020.

A review of technology and design practice

"One of the important aspects of industrial design is the impact of new technologies that impose new solutions for product design. Accordingly, each of my projects, in the preparatory phase, involved researching new technologies and applying them in design. However, in many of my design concepts I have found new technological solutions. As a classic example, in this sense, is the development of computers. Since the first bulky, today we have miniature (PC) that are at the same time much faster in data processing and storage. These drastic changes are due to the development of new technologies and methods of production.

The point of this exhibition is that changes in technological terms affect the solutions of industrial designers and vice versa, design ideas can influence technological change: it has happened in the past, it is happening in the present and will be present in the future. I would therefore suggest young industrial designers to closely monitor the technological advances in the world. Unlike the "small" exhibition n HDD gallery two years ago, when all the media were present, this time TV, newspapers and magazines did not come! At the time of the opening of the exhibition in Croatia there was a big strike by educators, so I suspect that the media were busy with this vital topic. However, one, but valuable article was published in the blog Vizkulturo under the name: Industrial design tailored to man, authored by Sonja Leboš.

Photo: Barbara Blasin

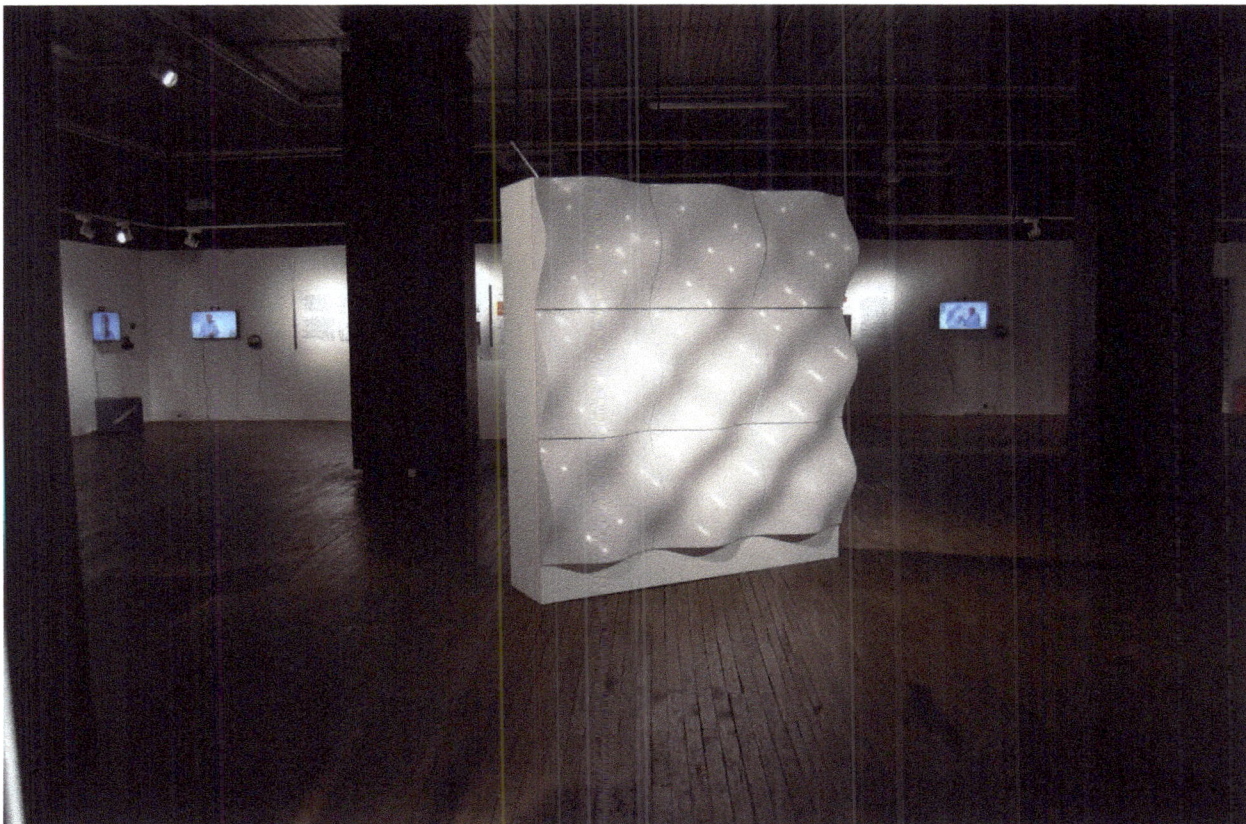

Sculptra wall: Photo D Grunwald

Chairs Elips, Sculptra wall, Photo D. Grunwald

Chairs Elips, Photo D. Grunwald

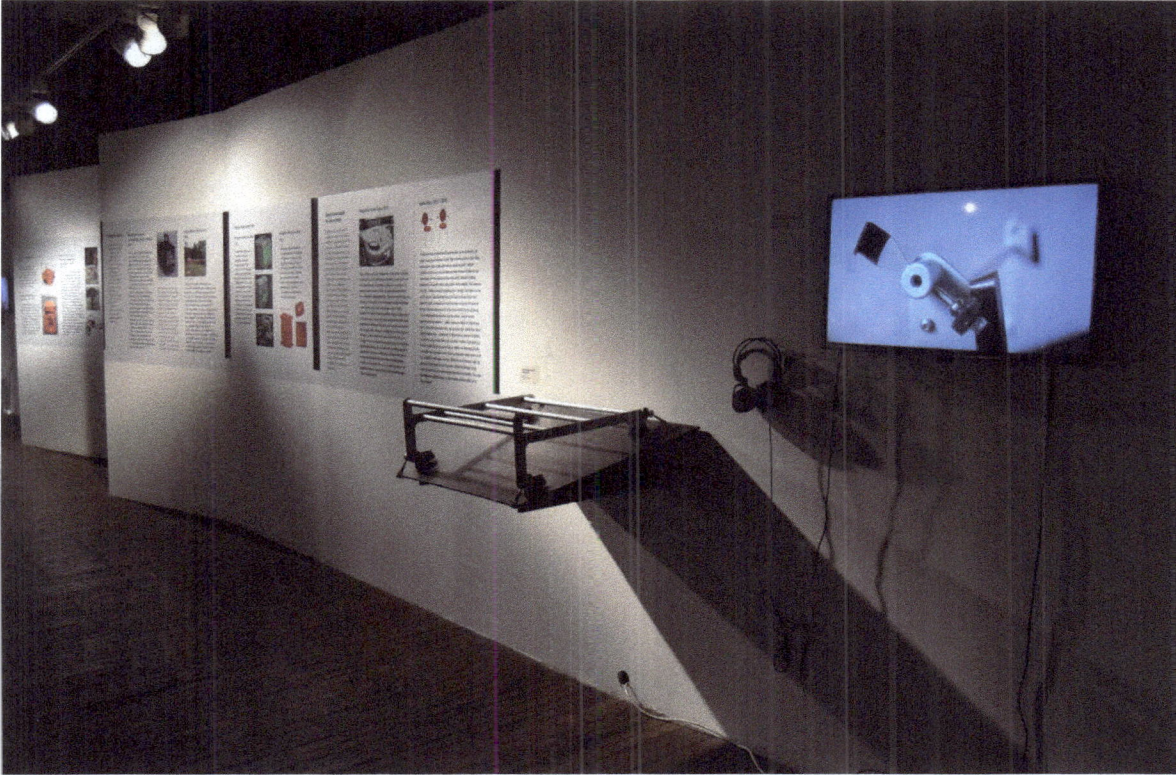

Rack for Porsche Boxster, Photo D. Grunwald

Electronic calculators for TRS, Foto Barbara Blasin

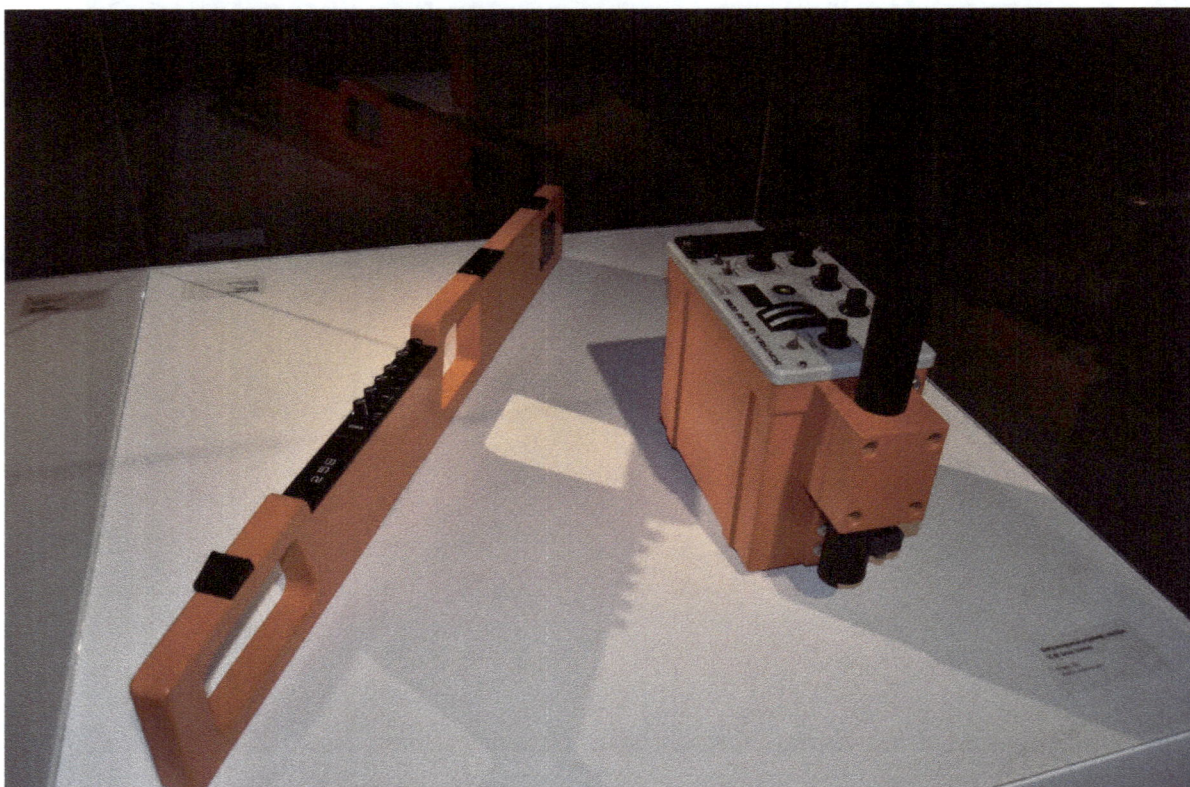

Geophysical instruments: Geonics EM38 and Scintrex Genie, redeiver, Foto D. Grunwald

The exhibition was conceived and textual portion was done by Marko Golub and Koraljka Vlajo while Barbara Blasin processed the exhibition graphically.

Koraljka Vlajo and Marko Golub, curators of the exhibition, Barbara Blasin, setup and graphic design

The comments from the book of impressions from the exhibition at TMNT

You thrilled me to the immense pleasures of watching your exhibition; I knew there was a self-contained "devil-sage" in you, but not to the extent that I've now realized. I congratulate you on all your feats and successes, and I want your life to continue to be exciting and beautiful, well done, I'm so happy for your happiness, your satisfaction after all the effort and everything you've had to deal with in years past, but the justice and modesty you've been boasting have done their part. I congratulate you with all my heart and I want you to enjoy the well-deserved "glory". A big kiss from me! Well done, hooray!

Dr. Jaja Tomasković, Zane, school colleague

A beautiful exhibition, it shows how the design of the same designer developed in time, from student work to mature creations. Good job!

Signature unreadable.

 Finally a famous designer and made him a well-deserved exhibition. Unfortunately the good ones go out of the country because they won't be allowed to work here. Congratulation Davor!

 Ana Jelavić

This exhibition is the most complete presentation of all that has been presented so far by this talented and extremely successful designer from our premises. A beautiful picture of the development path, which also shows that in addition to talent and will, persistent work is often required with thorny obstacles. Congratulations!

 Zvonko Kuharić

I am delighted to have been present at significant events related to your work and thus had the opportunity to know your life path and professional achievements. This third, comprehensive exhibition at TMNT. could certainly be stimulating for young people, especially in these our spaces. If everyone were so responsibly, boldly and diligently developing their talents, from God, the world would look different.

Palma Orlović-Leko, PhD

Your exhibition was an indication of what can be done with your life if you're persistent and have the guts to face all the obstacles. In doing so, you must have a solid vision that will guide you when, despite your undeniable talent, you doubt your strength. You had it all, and I congratulate you on that. I know your activities aren't the end, because the restlessness in you won't let you. I wish you a lot of success in that.

Marija Tuga Neral

Industrial design tailored by man

Author: Sonja Leboš for Vizkultura

Industrial design seems in our society as a syntagma from some ancient past. A visit to the exhibition of Davor Grünwald entitled: Industrial Design in the context of technology, which can be viewed in the Technical Museum, Nikola Tesla until 1. February 20, 2020, it reveals to us, unfortunately, that this is only the case here, in a country where the industry is thoroughly destroyed, so even industrial design doesn't make much sense. But for now, as we suffer from this state of affairs, the objects exhibited in this exhibition, which are kept in the foundations of the Technical Museum and the Museum of Arts and Crafts, show that the city, which now boasts the most sausages in advent stands. could be raised (if there were any coherent management) and some very interesting museum of industrial design.

Exhibition "Industrial **Design** in the Context of Technology" by D. Grünwald, TMNT / photo: Boris , .
.. Cvjetanović

Exactly fifty years ago, in 1969. In Croatian industrial design (let's point out, however, truth for will, then in the Yugoslav federation) got a chance for a fresh start. As Feđa Vukić writes in his, Century of Croatian design, 1997., one wing of this new momentum of industrial design in the Socialist Republic of Croatia represents the transition of Vladimir Robotić from the Center for Industrial Design to the Design-Bureau of Rade Končar, and the second wing of the new beginning is marked by the return from Vienna of our first graduated industrial designer – Davor Grünwald.

Davor Grünwald, born 1943., he has been a peculiar figure, who has allowed his profession to become his life's calling, i.e., he has allowed his design practice to erase the boundaries between work and leisure. Judging by the satisfaction he emanates from when he talks about the objects he has shaped, talking about colors, housings, ergonomics, but also economics, Grünwald devoted himself very early to his work to such an extent that he very rarely made compromises about what this work should be, without alienating that work, either by himself, nor by those who would use it as a finished product. Whether he used his mother-in-law's oven to experiment with new materials, or spending his spare time in his own garage building prototypes to prove his superiority that he was right, this designer did not mind to show his stubbornness, which he claims is vital to the profession of (industrial) designer. However, the path he has crossed shows that such a choice is not always sprinkled with rose petals, but in his case, the persistence and stubbornness of proving that he is right have paid off well. As a gift when he retired, Grünwald gave himself a Porsche Boxster. Even such a car, which many would hold as sacred, Grünwald had a need to fix: often with his wife, he goes on trips from which they return with baskets full of fruit or antique furniture, he "fixed" the Porsche Boxter with a rack mounted on the back trunk. But the retired industrial designer still has a multitude of ideas – one is also intended for the safety of cyclists. Driven by the fact that motorists are approaching too close to cyclists, he has made a stick to keep their distance. The designer is impossible to retire: he is also intrigued by the chair, because, as he says "there are a million" different types of chairs in the world, but I was interested to find out how to make one for which it is no need to invest in tools, which contains only cheap materials, and still works well and looks good" (from the exhibition catalogue below).

.   Rack for Porsche Boxter, 2013. (left); Chairs Ellips (right) / photo: Boris Cvjetanović

But let's go back half a century: how did it all start?

After returning from Vienna, where he graduated with a degree in industrial design from the Academy of Applied Arts, Grünwald is looking for his first job in Zagreb. He chooses the Factory of Calculating Machines (imagine, we had that!) with which he will collaborate for the next five years, in his capacity as an independent artist-designer, i.e. through his own design studio, which he called Prodesign. Why the Computer Machine Factory right now? "It was close to my house and I found it quite interesting." The first product he worked on was the Calcorex mechanical calculator, a robust and heavy machine to which he built a new housing in injection plastic and introduced thinner metal components, making the object greatly lighter. That's how Calcorex 403 was created, and the entire Calcorex line, thus extended life by another decade. The power of good design!

Grünwald then developed electronic calculators (some components, such as transistors, had to be imported from the United States, but perhaps that is why Yugoslavia had the opportunity to market such products in Eastern European countries), devising the concept, as he puts it, of "strong ergonomic characteristics".

So he designed the Index battery calculator keyboard, it builds up the round shape on a square key base, thus avoiding errors that occur by randomly pressing the adjacent key. This extremely intelligent design never arrived in the West, precisely because of the orientation of Yugoslavia towards the Eastern European market, but also the huge (probably unsparing) competition in the west (let's just mention Sharp, Toshiba or Texas Instruments).

Calculators for the Factory of Calculator Machines / Photo: Boris Cvjetanovic

In addition to the Factory of Calculating Machines, in the period 1969-1974. Grünwald also works with Prvomajska , where he works on machine tools such as sharpener, lathe, etc. making modifications, and here Grünwald focused on ergonomic improvements, to make the machine's handling as practical as possible, but also – more humane, adapting the machine to man, not the other way around. Of course, such an approach required industrial ethnography, talking to workers and studying their approach to the machine, the way the body was used and the position of the body when working. So he noticed that it made no sense for people to sit on wooden boxes while they were working (!),so he designed chairs with backrests that had room to move their elbows. While

Bernardi and Richter designed chairs for comfortable seating, Grünwald made sure the workers were as comfortable as they worked.

For the redesign of the series of machine tools for Prvomajska Davor Grünwald was awarded the Golden Plaque at the large Machine Fair in Leipzig in 1973. In 1974, the City of Zagreb Award was won by Grünwald.

On the occasion of the latter, Bernardo Bernardi wrote of Grünwald: "By forming a family of machine tools for the Prvomajska factory from Zagreb, he took the only correct path – through a detailed analysis of all those sensitive conditions arising from the man-machine relationship. In this work, Grünwald has demonstrated that he is capable of sensing and combining elements of ergonomic analysis, technical and technological conditions with the complex requirements of high operational functionality. But his intervention doesn't stop at the technical limit. With exceptional sensibility for artistic phenomena, he was able to turn all the possibilities of rational instrumentation and the demands of technical necessity transform into visual reality and harmonious artistic unity. In this way, these machines become an essential element of the overall atmosphere of the working. In 1975, unhappy with the conditions of work, but also by the requirement that as a manager (it was briefly obvious) to join the Union of Communists, Grünwald left for Canada. In Canada, there were few, only two dozen, in Canada at the time, according to Grünwald.' As he says, "What I learned in TRS and Prvomajska, I applied it in Canada". Instructive, isn't it?

What is interesting about his highly successful career is that he changed jobs quite often, and very often it was precisely because of incoherent demands of employers (e.g. in Delphax he was fired illegally), because "the head of marketing was a former CIA officer, and was very sensitive to red color", so he resented for using red colour when designing the logo).

. Sculptra wall and digital underground radar for Sensors & Software Inc., TMNT / photo: Boris Cvjetanović

In Canada, Grünwald also worked for a company called Prodesign for a while, the name as a design studio that he founded himself in Zagreb. There he designs a pop-up stand, an advanced concept for that time, and cooking utensils. After various complications, the trajectory of the search for work takes him to Winnipeg 1978. where he has designed a tractor for the agricultural company Versatile. In the early 1980s, he got a job in Toronto, as a draftsman at Scintrex Instruments, Research and Exploration. Here he designs its first geophysical instrument, Genie, for underground exploration (geophysics in Canada are highly developed, due to the intense exploitation of the richest of the Earth's crust).

As he sought a place as a home designer and a higher salary and was rejected, Grünwald left Scintrex and practically found a job the next day at Delphax, founded by a "runaway IBM group", which at that time began developing fast printers. And yet his tendency to find better ergonomic solutions has come to the forefront, improving machines. For Delphax he developed, as well, new corporate identity. But even in Delphax, for the reasons mentioned above, does not stay long, so he goes to the Geonics, where he continues to work with geophysical instruments and where he remains until the 2008. Perhaps the most interesting instrument from this period is the EM38 Conductivity Meter. Since 1985, the instrument he has had the opportunity to redesign several times. This instrument has a body made of cherry wood, a material with the lowest coefficient of stretching.

Conductivity meter EM38, 1985 and Scintrex Genie, receiver / photo: Boris Cvjetanović

Everything here is only part of the exhibition signed by Marko Golub, Koraljka Vlajo and Barbara Blasin, and to which especially charm is given by video interviews with Grünwald himself who speaks directly about his products (the author of the video interview is Marko Golub). The catalogue of the exhibition, which gives an insight not only into Grünwald's work, but also the socio-political context of the companies for which he worked, and thus the cultural context of the objects he created, was superbly conceived by the cuthors of the exhibition Marko Golub and Kcraljka Vlajo, and designed by Barbara Blasin.

This is an exhibition to take yourself, children, grandchildren, or younger relatives, and to remember some days when this country could have given some essential work experience and professions other than medicine, before moving their bread belly to some distant lands in search of a fairer salary for their work. , as well as the necessity to think with own head. It's a real exhibition at the right time.

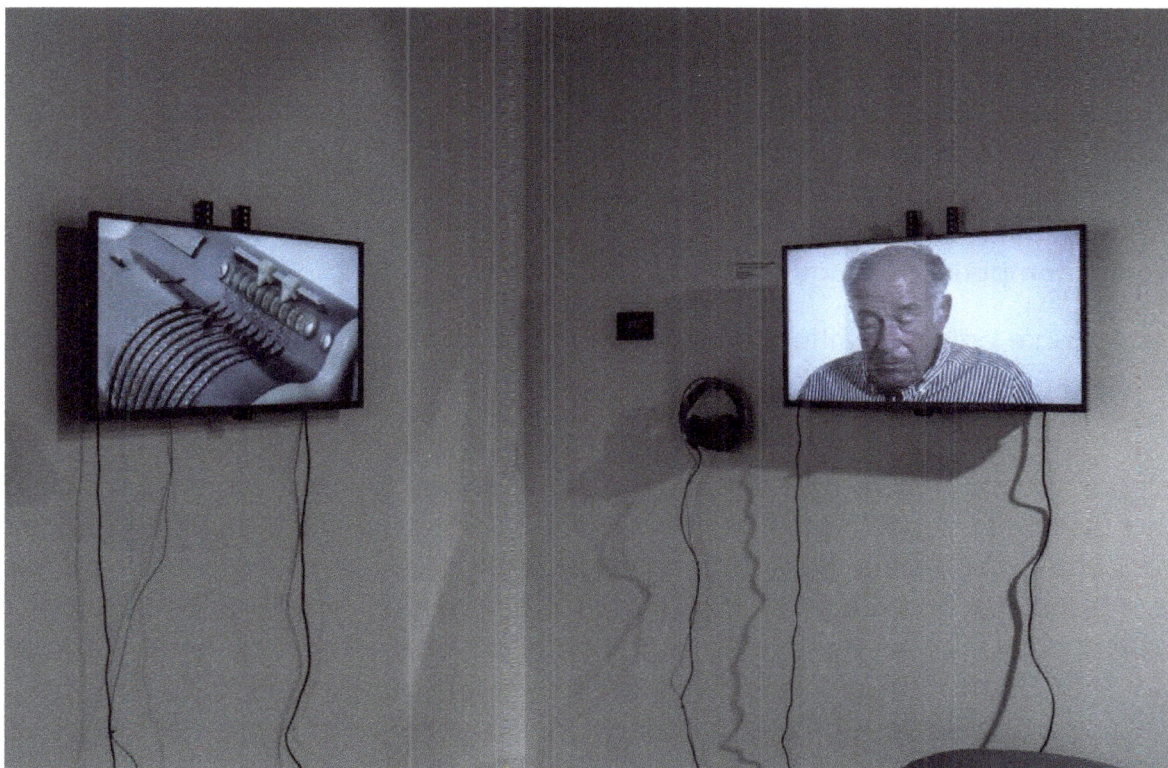

Video interview with Davor Grünwald / Photo: Boris Cvjetanović

Gorislav Keller, dedicated a text in the journal: Creative Communications, under the title Why Did Davor Grünwald Left?

Dear Mrs. Leboš, Marko Golub informed me of your: "Beautiful text, very commendcble and very extensive" – INDUSTRIAL DESIGN TAILORED BY MAN. I read the article and remained literally speechless. You've made me excited to the immense delights, reading that text. You have connected all the written, spoken materials in the context of the environment – just wonderful! You're a virtuoso; it's a wonderful Christmas present! I wish you a pleasant Christmas holiday and many more such beautiful articles in Nova 2020.
Davor Grünwald

Comments on my professional presentation

"Davore, excellent story, I did not believe it was possible, but you had to go through the bitter experiences of the capitalist system. However, you have a personal satisfaction that your problems stem from your competitiveness, since you're a good designer. You got away with it because in skirmishes you were brave and persistent. Anyway, congratulations! This extended version of your work CV further confirms that you are a good designer, above all dedicated to developing your talent, and that's why you're successful. Your story should be published to our young people as an example in today's world of disturbed values in which it is not popular to create and work, which is the only true path to progress."
My classmate, graduate engineer Zvonko Kuharić

Like your other friends, and I read the text of your memoir in one breath. Yes, life writes the most interesting stories and yours is certainly in that category. I appreciate your talent, your expertise, your persistence, and above all that, despite all the challenges, you've stayed true to yourself. I also congratulate you on the honor shown to you by the Museum of Arts and Crafts (MUO) in Zagreb and the Design Exchange in Toronto by archiving your design works!
Branka Komparić, colleague

Memoirs are brilliantly written, concise, with lots of extremely interesting details, humor and honesty.
Jasna Lovrinčević, journalist

"I thank you most for your life story, which showed your business successes, most thanks to your creativity, high expertise, but also your exceptional confidence and willingness to cooperate. True during the realization of your projects, you more often had enemies among your associates and "superiors" than friends, ready to help; incentives and support, and you yourself courageously persevered on the path to success. Your high competencies result in real enthusiasm in projects and creating an excellent atmosphere for drawing up and realizing plans. However, there are people who at some point express due diligence, and at another point, depending on their special interests, treat them as flaws. You made the right decisions on your own and accepted or cancelled further cooperation in situations that hindered the realization of your projects. Thank you so much for the hard work and time you put into writing the memoir "My Story." The title itself also points to your gift of writing and literacy with which you have compiled this extremely interesting text. It is a brilliantly conceived and carefully written text in which you have connected in the most beautiful way two realities, professional and business, especially in us unknown foreign world. All of these projects are described as plastic, and although they are not visually displayed, which would contribute to the idea of their design, the very insight into the results of your research and projects confirms that they are designed at the highest level. It's just surprising the variety of the thematic projects you've been doing, reflecting the excellence of your design abilities. For this very purpose, I hope that you will inform us of your further projects and support them with imaging material in order to bring your professional and creative achievements closer together.   (Note: Zvonko and Vlado Kuharić are nephews of Kardinal Kuharić)

My classmate, academic painter, Vlado Kuharić

Way to go, Davor! You're consistent, thank you for the collegial and public offering to the design profession. You're doing good things and I'm happy that you will be included in the Museum of arts and crafts (MUO).
Graphic designer, Boris Ljubičić

"And now about your story...... I read it like a crime scene, in one breath! Really amazing, what life path and how you just clearly felt your life's calling and followed it with such unwavering conviction and dedication, well done!"
Master of Industrial Design, Ika Peraić

Now I've received your message and i've been literally speechless. You thrilled me to the immense pleasures of reading your texts; I knew there was a self-contained "devil-sage" in you, but not to the extent that I've now understood. I congratulate you on all your feats and successes and I want your life to continue to be exciting and beautiful, I hope we will soon meet and chat a little more about the old days of our high school lives. I'm very proud of my dear Davor again, well done, I'm so happy for your happiness, your satisfaction after all the hard work and everything you've had to deal with in years past, but the justice and modesty you boast has done its part. I congratulate you with all my heart and I want you to enjoy the well-deserved "glory", a big kiss from me! Well done, hooray!
Dr. Jaja Tomašković, Zane – school coll

Interview with Davor Grünwald, Croatian/Canadian industrial/product designer, ORIS magazine, 2020.

The conversation was conducted by Marko Golub and Koraljka Vlcjo

KV: In your speech when opening your exhibition at the Technical Museum, Nikola Tesla under the title: Davor Grünwald, industrial design in the context of technology, you mentioned "It is me!".

DG: Yes, this beautifully conceived exhibition depicts my half-century professional oeuvre. Well, of course, "It's me!" But I also shouted it in 1963. at an exhibition of Italian design at the Museum of Arts and Crafts (MUO) because then I was inspired for that profession , I did not know what was waiting for me.

 MG: In a conversation we had ahead of the exhibition we staged at the HDD Gallery 2017. You stated, "I am a 100% practitioner". What does that mean for you?

DG: The design theorist is my "counterbalance", which explains my work in a philosophical way. That's how that person makes me a kind of commercial. However, to survive in the world of corporations, there is no room for philosophy. My presentation design solutions have been always "to the point", clear, well-argument logical solutions expressed by vocabulary engineers, marketing experts and executives of corporations. For example, in the geophysical industry, there was no classical market research. The only feedback they had was the one from the field, and the clients came with requests for specific research. Small batches of products worked on that principle.

MG: Before you went to study design at the Academy of Applied Arts in Vienna, you studied electrical engineering in Zagreb for two years. Did that experience help you later as a designer?

DG: Yes, in fact, because for most of my career, I have been engaged in electronic instruments. At the university itself, the first two years were not much electronics, more theories, physics, mathematics, basics of electronics. But I still got some ideas on those foundations. Even before that, I was amateur in electronics, making single-bulb and two-bulb radios, and so I gained some ground, I knew how to talk to electrical engineers in factories. I understood their language and it helped me a lot.

MG: What was that breaking moment for you when you realized you wanted to do design?

DG: In fact Zvonimir Radić, "Diša" helped me a lot in my decision. He was director of the Center for Industrial Design (CIO), and a professor at the Academy, traveled a lot attending in congresses at the time when industrial design began to emerge. He had all the information in the "little finger." I recognized myself in the design after seeing an exhibition of Italian design at the Museum of Art and Crafts, I came to Radić and he just said to me, there's a school in Ulm, go there. And there's something about Vienna." However, I did not reach Ulm, I ended up in Vienna with Professor Franz Hoffmann. I had a very strong intuition when I saw this exhibition at the Museum, it was like lightning hit me, it was so strong, I couldn't resist and I just followed that instinct.

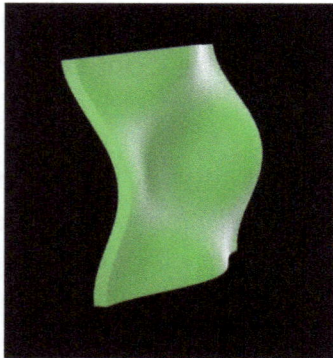

Sculptra, architectural module, 1964.

Sculptra application, camp Bunja, Croatia,

KV: In Vienna, an object has been created that accompanies you throughout your professional life – Sculptra.

DG: Then it was not yet called Sculptra, then it was only one small element (12 x 12 cm) which when multiplied can be connected vertically and cannot be horizontal. I remember the moment we got that task and the blank white paper in front of me in the second semester (1964). My colleagues already had some ideas, sharp corner solutions in the wood.

And then it dawned on me! The math was still in my head, so let's see if there's anything in that sinus and cosine. When the professor saw those little elements I made, he was thrilled.

KV: Sculptra was also exhibited at the New Tendency 3 exhibition in Zagreb.

DG: Yes, it was 1965. I made nine elements and arranged them by displaying four different combinations of mergers. After the exhibition, I came to pick up that exhibit of mine. I was told it was stolen. There was no documentation left of it, just my word. I later called the Sculptra, protected the design and the name. It became my three-dimensional emblem.

KV: How would you describe Sculptra?

Sculptra is not subject to industrial design, have never claimed it. It's the only abstract sculptural form I've made in my career. Sculptra form is abstract, simple, attractive, natural and associate comfort and positivity. It locks fresh, as if it was created now and not subject to any trends. It will remain unique and eternal in the world! Reflections of light on its rounded surfaces capture the view of the observer and awaken their interest in this exceptional design."

Redesign of mech. & electronic calculators designa for TRS, pocket calc., electr. Scale, 1969. – '74.

MG: During the period of operation in Croatia and Yugoslavia, you were most professionally tied to the Factory of Calculating Machines (TRS). What was the experience of working with them?

DG: Fantastic, I remember these relationships; starting with the director, through the engineers, mechanic engineers I collaborated with the redesign of the mechanical Calcorex 403. They welcomed me incredible nice. I was still a youngster at the time, 24 years old. I've been making things up for them, doing presentations, all the workers evaluating the proposed models. Then through these impressions and comments we came up with the products that were displayed in this exhibition. That extraordinary experience helped to me later in Canada.

MG: Can you describe the beginning of your collaboration with TRS?

DG: Simply, I came to TRS and said "I would like to speak to the director! I am an industrial designer, I have completed the Academy in Vienna and I want to offer my cooperation." And the director took me in. He knew who I was, the CIO had kind of prepared the terrain for me, and they were already operating everywhere, so thanks to them the factory directors already had some ideas about industrial design. And I had just come from Vienna and I was many times cheaper than them, I was competing, I was capitalistic/competitive in the socialist system and thus managed to get jobs.
TRS had a problem with old Calcorex, mechanical calculator, at the time, it wasn't selling

well, and the director asked me if there was anything I could do to extend its life. I suggested a redesign. I studied the old model in detail, I saw that the numbers on it could not be read, bad ergonomics, too hard, nothing worked well. Then I spoke to the engineers and I offered to make new casings in the injection plastic, they had excellent craftsmen who made tools for plastic. I also suggested replacing heavy metal components with thinner once. The black numbers are imprinted with a hot process in plastic. Now it was very readable. Besides, I saw this entire gray stuff in the offices – I suggested red for the new Calcorex, everything was gray in the offices. It all lived up and everyone loved that model that extended life by ten years.

MG: Within the 4-5 years you have worked with TRS, you have designed a solid number of electronic calculators.

DG: Yes, after Calcorex, TRS decided to develop and produce electronic calculators. In the west, powerful corporations were acting like Texas Instruments, Canon, Sharp... TRS hired electronic engineers and I immediately joined them, so I cooperated with them from the beginning. They started experimenting with the binary system, they were magnets and wires, they still didn't have transistors, they started with almost nothing. And then they got transistors from the United States, and that's how the serious electronics work started. That "rudimental" start inspired me for their new trademark.

MG: Did you have available information about similar electronic calculators from that time from other markets, some model that you could work on?

DG: At first I didn't because there wasn't a lot of information, yet we were in another, Eastern market and not the West. So mainly through my own thinking and analysis, I got my designs. I was not looking for something to compare with my ideas. Later, of course, I found other calculators, mainly in magazines and so I actually saw that I had done a good thing.

KV: You designed a very large number of new, different calculators in a very short time.

DG: TRS was aggressive on this issue. They saw that the only way they could survive. Its market was Russia and the Eastern Bloc, but still a very big market.

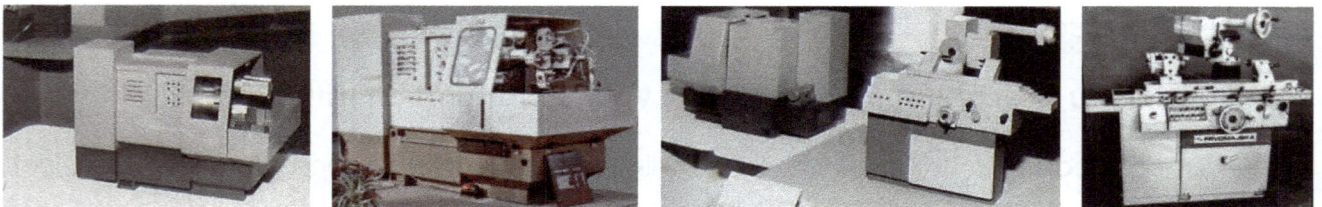

Redesign of machine tools for Prvomajska, models 1 : 10, 1970. – 1974

MG: Two other companies were important to you at the time - Prvomajska and "Jadran" Metal Furniture Factory.

DG: I entered Prvomajska in the same way as earlier in TRS. Through the door, boom, at the director's, "good day, I'm such and such, and can I help you?" I worked for very small fees, but it was important to me to have a product that I designed to show others. While I was working on machine tools for Prvomajska it was clear to me that there was a lot of room for improvements in ergonomics, that people work better with the machine, to better understand it, but also that the machine better "understands" them. Then I realized there was room for other improvements. The machines had very heavy cone bases, made of steel that was poured in the sand. I was going through their drives and watching them work, huge cranes, everything smoking and steaming. I've been thinking about some new method, because the machines are too heavy and clunky. I suggested that the bases should be made out of steel plates that are cut and welded, and they agreed. I had an incredible influence on them, they agreed on everything I suggested. So they made large lathes and sharpeners, and the bases for them from cut sheet metal. This approach was better because I had a surface on which all electronics and other components could be better mounted than on the sloped one. Anyway, I influenced on their production technology with, one which was much cheaper.

KV: For this redesign of machine tools you also received the City of Zagreb Award

DG: Yes I received this prestigious Award, 1973. for these machines. I was the youngest winner of that award by then. In the same year, these machines were given a Golden Plaque at the international fair in Leipzig. I applied an ergonomic study (Magisterial Work). All the elements that are touched by hand were important to be at the height of the bent arm, and those that are seen at eye level, because that is all logical. They didn't think so systemically. It was important to me that operators were well protected when working. The sharpener had a characteristic cone base, and one engineer told me it was because they wanted it to resemble a silhouette of a man! Imagine, it was an engineering answer to a very rational question! I told them, "Look, that's not how it works; I'm going to make it stable, visual and physical. I changed their color, too. Until then, they used a green Hammerschlag that was very ugly to me, so I asked them to change it – the base was dark brown, the upper part beige, and accents in other colors served to make the elements ergonomically distinguish with each other.

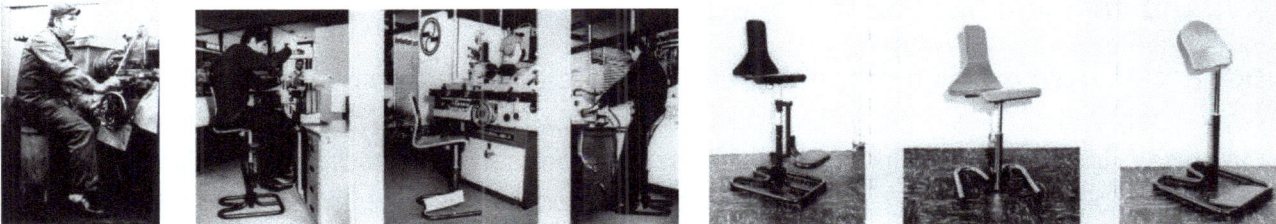

Industrial chairs for "Jadran" , 1970 - 1972

KV: Your cooperation with the Jadran came from your engagement in Prvomajska, right?

DG: Yes, I watched workers sit next to big machine tools on wooden boxes. I photographed these situations and concluded that I have to make for these people' chairs to sit on. I made chairs with a narrow backrest to smoothly move the elbows. For some reason the Director of the Jadran was in Prvomajska and saw the chairs, he asked who did this and so I came to him for an interview. He offered me the position of director of development, and I agreed, and I was developing the chairs further.

MG: And how formally did your studio Prodesign work?

 DG: I have to remember a little bit, because I wondered a lot... The factory of calculators, then Prvomajska, then the Jadran from which I left after three months, when I was told that I had to enlist in the Communist Party. That's when I founded Prodesign. I made a sign, in a circle as the ideal form, I presented compromises. Because every design is a compromise, a little of this, a little bit of that; it can't be 100% everything right. Compromise within the circle, it presented me as a professional, graphically/philosophically.

MG : Prodesign was also the reason why your activity was terminated here.

 I was an aggressive, professional. I didn't think about how a consultancy like that works. My studio was in my mother's apartment at Vodnikova Street. And I started working, until one day two cops came. 'You have an illegal company!' 'How?' Well, I work here. There's no secrets, no illegal...' 'No, no, no, we have to take all that away, everything you have here, and you can't work under that name or that way.' And so it all fell apart. 'If we find you in that situation one more time, you're going to jail.' And then I worked without that name. But, interestingly, I already had the status of a free profession that the state guaranteed me to work in that capacity.

KV: Maybe the problem was performing under the name Prodesign, not under own name?

DG: Yes, I was wrong to have a private consulting office in communism. They ruined my career in Croatia in 1974, when they abolished all the contracts I had with the factories. I come to talk, 'Ouch, we can't, Yugoslavia doesn't allow us to work with privates anymore.' I say, 'I have this status through a professional association; I have a legal right to work.' No, we can't. And so it all fell apart.

KV: And then you headed to Canada?

DG: E, then I told myself that somewhere in this world must be a place for me, where I can work freely without restrictions. Europe was closed at the time. They wouldn't let me go to Germany anymore. Switzerland was interesting; they already had good designers at that time. They didn't want me either. Australia is too far away, what I'm going to do there? So Canada has left. At the Canadian Embassy in Belgrade, the Ambassador told me 'Well, it's not exactly the situation....' And I say, 'Look, what I've been through here, it must be better there. It couldn't be any worse.'

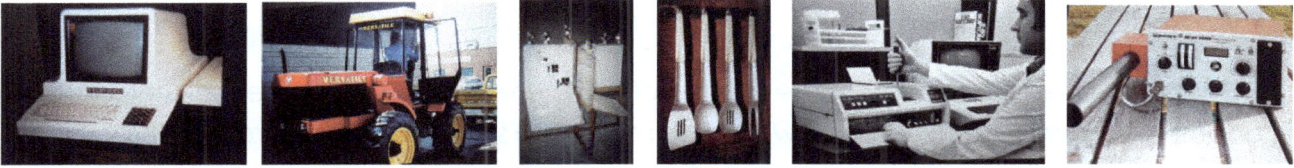

Computer, tractor, utensil, Genie geophysical instr. Atomic absorption instr. 1975. – 1981.

KV : And how did you start your career in Canada?

DG: I immediately joined the Industrial Designers Association, to get a little sense, to talk to these people a little bit. In many ways, I spread acquaintances and found out where, what and how. It was immediately clear to me that I had to get a job somewhere. Through the ads, I got a job at a factory that made electronics housings. I got in touch and they took me in, even though I didn't even know the U.S. measurement system yet. The co-owner was German, I spoke to him in German, I didn't even know English yet.

MG: How much has the design experience of the Yugoslav industry helped you there?

DG: Very much, I approached the companies in the same way. If I saw the potential for a job somewhere, I'd come to their door. So it worked similarly like in Zagreb. All these companies I worked for i found that way, they had no idea about industrial design. It's an identical thing. I became an educator and promoter again, and in Canada.

MG: You're constantly changing locations in the coming years, if I remember correctly. First very short Toronto, then Montreal, then Winnipeg, then Toronto permanently.

DG: Yes, after Toronto I came to Montreal, and after 6 months i was joined by my family, wife and daughter. At the time, Quebec wanted to secede from Canada, so the newcomers were much hounded. The restaurant didn't want to serve you if you didn't speak French, it was a very uncomfortable time. Then I worked for a Frenchman who accepted me, somehow we found ourselves. His consulting firm was also called Prodesign. However, he got me for a little money, even at one point he got a ticket for keeping me "in black." I realized I had to move on, that I couldn't survive there. I found an American industrial designer in Winnipeg who had his own bureau. That man was phenomenal. He's been arranging jobs, very fast with many factories all over Canada. He was a very good businessman. However, he was a veteran of the Vietnam War and occasionally had seizures. He'd get dressed in his military uniform and start with orders, by jelling; I was just waiting for him to pull out the knife. That was embarrassing. I stayed with him for a year, and then I left.

KV: You worked with him on tractor design for Versatile?

DG: I worked with him on a tractor, yes. We split up - he, I and another young designer, we each did our own version. Then the president of Versatile looked at these works. 'That's what we're going to do!' and pointed to my solution. And he added 'It has a European look and we are interested in selling in Europe.'

KV : And after Winnipeg ?

DG: I realized Winnipeg was "in the middle of nowhere." There was some industry, but it wasn't enough. I knew I had to settle down in Toronto. There's the industry, there's everybody, it's English territory. I got a job with a colleague at the Association, he had a well-established business, so I worked with him for six months and let my tentacles see where I was and what I was. I came across a head-hunter, an employment company, and through them I got the job as a draftsman in Scintrex.

Ion fast printers: horizontal, vertical, office - exhibition system, 1980. – 1984.

MG : Then begins cooperation with Scintrex, i.e. your entry into the geophysical industry?

DG: Yes, yes. With Scintrex, it was interesting, too. I said to myself, okay, I'm going now as a draftsman, so I'm going to show who I am really later. They sat me down with the other draftsman's in the big room. I've done my own thing, doing color sketches, models in cardboard. Everyone's watching, both the draftsman and the boss. 'Well, what's that? You do it quite differently than the others.' That's when I admitted I was actually an industrial designer. Then the president of the company called me, and he said, "Oh, we appreciate that very much. You just keep doing it." I say "Yes, but I'd like my salary a little bit lager for that and the position of industrial designer",   "no, no, your salary is fine. Let's not talk about it. But continue   what you do."

MG: Are some of the important products of Scintrex already produced?

DG: Yes, yes. Then there is a very interesting geophysical product that was worn on the back, a transmitter. The second man was carrying a receiver 20 yards away. Magnetic field flows through the earth and if they encounter something conductive (For example, a metal barrel with toxic waste), it will distort and the computer will record the location (GPS) and the depth in which something is located. This was the first geophysical device treated by industrial design.

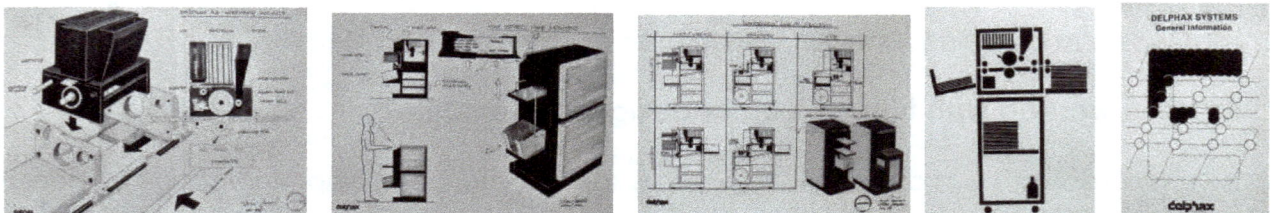

Sketches related to the development of fast ion printer, 1980. – 1994.

KV: That was Genie?

DG: Yes, Genie's was the name, right. It was actually a phenomenal product. I've really worked hard to do it right, that it is ergonomically correct, it can be comfortable to carry, that it can be easily handled, that the battery can be replaced quickly, etc. And 've been doing some other instruments, like the Instrument that analyzes traces of noble materials. And that product was successful. Then I won the prestigious Canada Design Award for Genie.

KV: Were you still employed at Scintrex or did you do it as an external associate?

DG: I started genie at Scintrex, but I left when the company's president refused to raise my salary. I got a job at Delphax, and then Scintrex invited me to continue working with Genie. For a couple of years, I had a good salary, double income, a job in Delphax and income from Scintrex.

KV: What did employment at Delphax look like?

DG: I was hired by the head of the mechanical department, where the engineers were developing a new printer based on a single patent. Until then, the printers worked on the basis of a laser. But this was an ion deposition technology for which the printer was just developing; the principle had not yet been applied in practice. I soon realized that the engineers were headed in the wrong direction. They imagined the paper entering the machine, coming down and then coming out. And it's a printer of a large amount of documents. The start of the process was good, but in the end you have to bend to the floor to lift that amount of heavy paper. I realized it couldn't be that way. The whole process must flow horizontally; the input and output must be in the same level (ergonomics!). Engineers didn't immediately accept that. I fought them for a long time and concluded that I had to deal with it "in a partisan way." In my garage I made a model 1:1, "borrowed" the components at work, installed everything into the model and one day brought it to the office of the president of the company. I came in early that Monday, put everything in his office and waited. 'Holy cow! Who did this?' That's when I came in his room and explained to him why I did it. He immediately put me in a position where I could influence the development of printers. He gave me space to make models; he gave me whatever needed. Since then, I've been head of concepts at Delphax. I've been developing ideas, working on cardboard, paper, foam plates.

And then came the news that Delphax's head office was moving to America, to Boston. There was talk of Xerox being behind it. I agreed to go to Boston, but with the family staying in Toronto and the company paying me once a month to go to Toronto on a plane plus rent a car. In Boston, however, something happened after three months. My boss called a meeting, and he said: 'Why did you make our trademark red?' I made a corporate identity back in Toronto and it was accepted. 'Well don't you know that American traditional color is blue?' I said to him, 'Mr. Mastedino, this is still a Canadian company, and the Canadian color is red. Look at the Canadian flag: "The man got red face, not a blue! He rushed out. The next day, he kicked me out of the company. Delphax's office in Toronto claimed I quit verbally, but I was expelled. That's a big difference because if I'd quit, I'd have to pay $10000 - 20000 to pay back what they've invested in me. I sued them for wrongful dismissal for no valid reason. The process took two years; I got a lot of money for it. Well, that's such a nice story to tell now. And at that moment it was very nerve wrecking.

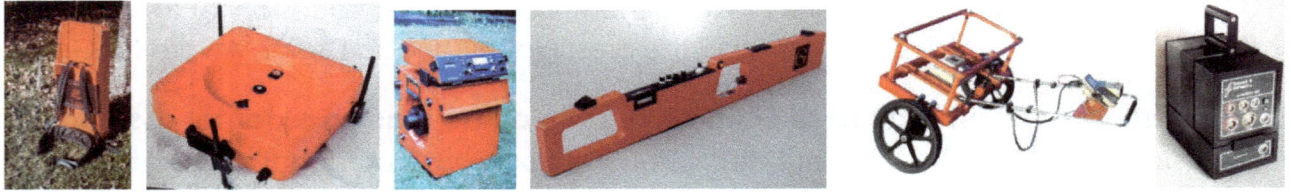

Genie, antenna, winch, EM38 and EM61 geophysical instr. Radar geof. Instrument, 1984. – 1994.

MG: But after that you get a job at Geonics and it then last until retirement?

DG: No, I've been scraping for a while. The Delphax guys threatened me with: 'You're not going to get a job in Canada anymore.' Because when someone's interested in me he or she is looking for the past references. And Delphax made me very bad; I didn't get the job for two years. That's when I met a colleague from Athletic Club, where I was a runner, who was vice president of the Geonics.

KV: Colleague from Zagreb?

DG: From Zagreb, yes. Those are your school contacts. I didn't have any in Canada, but this one was. And he said: 'Look, we're developing geophysical instruments, and I'm aware they're not well designed.' He figured out who I was and offered me to work contractually on an electromagnetic device for testing the quality of the soil.

KV: EM 38?

DG: EM 38, yes. 'Look what you can do with that.' That's how I started, as an outside consultant. They had a wooden board on which the electronics were scattered all over the place; it's a horror that it was. I arranged it all for them, coordinated it all, and applied ergonomics and then I got an offer to work for them in a permanent job.

KV: After that you made a whole series of instruments for them?

DG: Yes, but the geophysical industry generally did not know about industrial design. There's a concentration of these industries in Toronto, so I've been touring them and working for them on the side. I've been coming to these companies and I've introduced industrial design to them for the first time. This colleague of mine, an athlete, later became president of Geonics, he shouldn't have known that I am working for other various geophysical companies, so I hid this like a snake its legs. And I made good money on the side. I worked for Sensors & Software, which used the radar method, and for Gem Systems, which used earth's magnetic field. Otherwise, Gem Systems was founded by engineer Ivan Hrvoić and led to world quality. He invented all these instruments, but he also lacked good design. The business relationship with him lasted 20 years, until I retired. Well, that's the story from Croatia and Canada.

DG: From Zagreb, yes. Those are your school contacts. I didn't have any in Canada, but this one was. And he said: 'Look, we're developing geophysical instruments, and I'm aware they're not well designed.' He figured out who I was and offered me to work contractually on an electromagnetic device for testing the quality of the soil.

KV: EM 38?

DG: EM 38, yes. 'Look what you can do with that.' That's how I started, as an outside consultant. They had a wooden board on which the electronics were scattered all over the place; it's a horror that it was. I arranged it all for them, coordinated it all, and applied ergonomics and then I got an offer to work for them in a permanent job.

KV: After that you made a whole series of instruments for them?

DG: Yes, but the geophysical industry generally did not know about industrial design. There's a concentration of these industries in Toronto, so I've been touring them and working for them on the side. I've been coming to these companies and I've introduced industrial design to them for the first time. This colleague of mine, an athlete, later became president of Geonics, he shouldn't have known that I am working for other various geophysical companies, so I hid this like a snake its legs. And I made good money on the side. I worked for Sensors & Software, which used the radar method, and for Gem Systems, which used earth's magnetic field. Otherwise, Gem Systems was founded by engineer Ivan Hrvoić and led to world quality. He invented all these instruments, but he also lacked good design. The business relationship with him lasted 20 years, until I retired. Well, that's the story from Croatia and Canada.

| Geophysical "Bird" | Wine Barrel | Ellipse Chairs | Control Device |

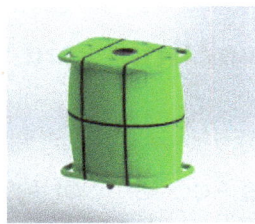

KV: In retirement, you continue to work. You're not going to give up! What's that stimulating you and what have you been working on?

DG: I'm working on objects without an industrial background, something I need. So I designed the rack for the Porsche Boxster I've driven since 2008 - a gift to myself for retirement. A very practical supplement for an extra suitcase or whatever.

I also designed the Ellipse chair. I was just wondering if I could make a chair different from a "few million" chairs, using CNC technology, without investing in tools, without welding and without screws.

Elips chairs in laminated wood, painted and hard wood, Ash

These are now hobby type activities that amuse me and satisfy me at that retirement age.

Davor Grünwald, 76

Biography of Davor Grünwald

After he completed his High school education 1962., he studied electronics at University of Zagreb. Got his diploma in Vienna 1968, from the Academy of Applied Arts, Department for Industrial Design. Stayed nine months longer at the Institute for Industrial Design and earned his Master degree on the theme: Ergonomics of Machines tools. With this he became the first formally educated Industrial designer in Croatia, Yugoslavia.

In 1969 returned to Zagreb and helped establish the Industrial Design Department at ULUPUH (Croatian Association of Applied Art). Got his freelance status and worked from his studio named PRODESIGN. During that time, he designed electronic calculators, tubular chairs, machine tools for which he received the 1973 Town of Zagreb Award. Was the youngest recipient at 30 years of age! 1972. He initiated YU-DIZAJN award at Zagreb fair. Unfortunately, in 1974 the communists prevented him to work for State factories (private enterprise was not permitted in communist Yugoslavia) so he immigrated to Canada 1975.

During the first four years in Canada, he lived in Montreal and Winnipeg and finally sank roots in Toronto in 1979. While he was working in freelance capacity or short engagements, he designed a variety of products, such as:

During the first four years in Canada, he lived in Montreal and Winnipeg and finally sank roots in Toronto in 1979. While he was working in freelance capacity or short engagements, he designed a variety of products, such as: tractor, computer console, geophysical "bird", geophysical radar system, collapsible wine barrel (BiB), trunk rack for Porsche Boxster and minimalistic chair Elips etc.

During the first four years in Canada, he lived in Montreal and Winnipeg and finally sank roots in Toronto in 1979. While he was working in freelance capacity or short engagements, he designed a variety of products, such as: tractor, computer console, geophysical "bird", geophysical radar system, collapsible wine barrel (BiB), trunk rack for Porsche Boxster and minimalistic chair Elips etc.

While he was employed with fast computer printers company Delphax (Ion Deposition Technology) 1980. till 1985. his aesthetic/ergonomic solutions have been noticed. 1983. received prestigious Canada Design Award for one geophysical instrument, Genie, designed for Scintrex.

From 1985. till 2012. he was employed with geophysical company Geonics for which he designed instruments and equipment, giving additional value to the products, by applying functional, aesthetic and ergonomic elements. With this he raised the products quality by the industry, which did not know anything about industrial design.
In 1995. he published article under the name: "Design of Products of Limited Production and Distribution", in ICSID NEWS 4/95. Then, the ICSID Industrial Design Definition was stating that Industrial Design is applied on "Mass produced products" only. He proposed that the ID definition should be extended to "Limited produced products" as well. Most of his designs belong to this category. 70% of world production are of this kind! World Design Organisation (WDO), former ICSID, accepted this proposal 2015.

From 1990. – 2000. he was vice-president of AMCA, Association of ex students of Croatian Universities and was creator of visual aspects of Gaudeamus magazine.
Since his arrival in Canada 1975 was one of Directors of Canadian Industrial Design Association.
He has been invited 2015. to archive his professional opus in Museum of Art and Craft in Zagreb (Muzej za umjetnost i obrt, MUO), on Boris Ljubičić recommendation.

Retrospective exhibit was organized in autumn 2017. in Zagreb in HDD Gallery under the name: Davor Grünwald Retrorama of Industrial Design, 1964 - 2008. and they published his small Monograph.

In December 2017 he received a Life Achievements Award from ULUPUH. It was sponsored by the City of Zagreb Assembly.
In May 2018. the exhibit from Zagreb has been installed in Split together with Boris Ljubičić graphic design exhibit.
His digital version of professional opus has been presented and archived in Canada Design Museum, Design Exchange in Toronto.

In November 2019. he had exhibit under the title: Davor Grünwald, Industrial Design in the Context of Technology, in Technical Museum Nikola Tesla (TMNT) in Zagreb.
He is a member of ULUPUH, Association of Croatian Applied Artists,   HDD, Association of Croatian Designers and ACIDO, Canadian industrial design Association
He has been included in Croatian Bibliographic and Art encyclopedia's.

 Davor Grunwald's opus is a part of the Croatian and Canadian design tradition and heritage.

Collected "thumbnails" from the life of Davo Grünwald

. **Granddad Josip, Granny Milka,**   **Daddy Mladen**   **Sister Mirna and Davor,**   **Mama Maja, Mirna and Davor**

The Monster

I spent the second and third years of my life with my uncle and aunt in Pitomača. It took that long for my mother to heal with the help of a psychiatrist and doctors after the tragic death of my father. He was killed in 1944 when the partisans blew up a train they believed to be full of German officers. He was 32 years old and my mother was 27. I have this vision of a courtyard with a huge tree in the middle of it, on one side there are farm buildings and on the other there is a small house. There were birds, entire flocks of them, that would often perch in the tree's branches and my uncle would take pellet gun...Boom! I knew that we would be eating bird stew that evening.
The winter was harsh that year. Dry snow, a good one meter deep, had fallen. Our only mode of transportation was a large sled pulled by two strong horses. I was seated mid-bench, between my uncle and the coachman, wrapped up in blankets. The smell of horses was intense and I liked it. Two huge-hunched horses danced to the rhythm of the bells attached to their heads. "Dzia!" yelled the coachman and the sled flew along a country road covered in packed snow. The sled abruptly stopped on a hill. The coachman struck the horses hard with his whip and cursed loudly, but it did not help to move the sled. On the edge of the horizon a black mass was growing increasingly larger every passing moment. The coachman grabbed me and threw me in the snow beside the road. I fell on my back, forming a crater in the snow. I saw only the gray sky. In the next instant, a black monster, roaring thunderously, appeared above me and then I heard the sound...taca...taca. It was the sound of freight wagons. This is where my memory stops.

Early childhood

My mother had to be intensively treated for shock after her husband's death. When she recovered all her attention, she focused on us kids, the older sister and me. We got up at 5:00 a.m., took us to day care at the Oil Factory where she worked as a secretary, right-hard to the director. The factory was at the end of Branimir's street in Zagreb and there was a tram. There was no money for my toys. I made myself stuffed animals with cotton wool. From carpenter in the neighborhood, I brought scraps of wood, "built" cities. From the old ball bearings, I got from the Oil Factory, I made a few scooters at the carpenter. I was most important in the company of friends on the street – my scooter was the loudest !

The Fall

My mother's friends invited us to a village near Zagreb to collect hay. It was an opportunity to witness a traditional celebration and feast. There was little for us children to do. I observed how the villagers loaded the hay onto the wagon. The hay pile grew and grew. How much higher could it go? It seemed to me that the horses will not be able to pull the wagon. The villagers secured the hay with rope and sat us children atop the pile. The rural road was full of potholes and mud from the last rainfall. The wagon swayed left and right. The swaying sensation was more intense at the top of the hay pile. Suddenly, the wagon swayed violently and I fell into the mud below. I found myself in the unfamiliar position of a sprinter readying him for the 100 meter dash, my left leg bent at the knee and extended backward and the right leg forward. From the corner of my left eye I noticed a huge wooden wheel with a metal ring heading straight towards me. The wheel was closing in on my leg. It was going to crush my bone just below the knee and I could not move because of the mud! It all happened in a split second. The wheel passed over my leg and all I felt was a little pressure. The wagon passed by and I got up in disbelief. I was not hurt! I was 10 years old and I clearly understood what had just happened. I had been incredibly lucky that the weight of the wagon had shifted in the other direction just as the wheel had crossed over my leg. I could have lost half of my leg or spent the rest of my life limping. I would fall again in my lifetime. The wheel of life would cross over me and every time it did, I arose unhurt and continued further.

Supetar, 1966. D. Grünwald

Drowning

The river Sava is flowing through Zagreb. The beach on river Sava was the only place one could cool up from the summer heat around fifties last century. I was eight years old when I went with my older sister Mirna to that place. The "pool" was constructed from wood and tight up at the coast. Water was flowing through grills. The boys, of my stature, were spraying the girls with water. I decided to join them. I swigged with my arm and I lost my balance. The bottom of the pool was slippery, from water weeds. I sunk under the surface and the strong river current "glued" me onto the grills. I could not free myself! I remember seeing the legs of the other swimmers and the sunshine penetrating the surface – how to free myself? In that moment somebody grabbed me by my swimming trunks and pulled me up. That was my sister who recognized me by my red swimming trunks.

Lovran, 1962, D. Grünwald

The runner

I was attending the First Gymnasium at Roosevelt square in Zagreb. The Second Gymnasium was vice versa scheduled and the Fourth and Fifth on the right side. Now days, this is a famous Mimara Museum. Track and field terrene was behind this building and was popular called Srednjoskolsko. Very often we had track and field competitions. I could hardly wait for my discipline, 1000 meters. I was always winning, the strategy I had I was running conservatively, but the last 150 meters I would switch into "fifth gear" and regularly left my colleagues 20 meters behind. It felt good the attention I was receiving from my peers. I become a member of track and field club Mladost at the Sava River. I was training hard and sometimes we would go to tunnel at the base of the Medvednica mountain and we would run to the top. My best time was 24 minutes. Last year it took me 2 hours. We were attending track and field competition all over Yugoslavia. Now when I think about these days it was excellent preparation for a life. I developed perseverance and competitor's spirit. It was important to tray arrive first. If I did not succeed I congratulated to the better one and hoping to win by the next occasion.

Strumica, Macedonia, 1970, D. Grünwald

Yin and Yang

In my sixteen years of age, I experienced the moment of inspiration. Everything in the world is based on balance. The proof of that I found in oriental philosophy by the name Yin and Yang which says that everything contain Yin and Yang. These are two opposites with complementary energies. They are completely different, but dependable in the world of nature. Natural disasters happened when the balance of the forces which hold the system, collapse. The communism did not prevail since it was based on one political system and dictatorship. Democracy spreads around the world because is based on balance of political parties and human rights.

From that revelation came that Industrial Design is sort of Yin and Yang of influencing components in the development of the new product.

In the sand

Vanja and I have grown up in the same street in Zagreb, Vodnikova street. Her father built playground for kids in the backyard. I have often come to play with her brother with whom I went to school together in Meduličeva street. We were building fortresses in the sand and little Vanja would come and destroyed them. I met Vanja many times on the street and observed her from my third floor window. When she arrived at teenage years she becomes slander, elegant, very pretty young lady.

I left for Vienna, Austria to study Industrial Design. I was in my third year. I was visiting Zagreb quite often in my old Citroen. By one such occasion Vanja's father has approached me. He told me that he worked for several years in Libya and put on the side some money for Vanja's education in Vienna at my Academy. Of course I agreed to help. The mother of one of my female college agreed to take Vanja to stay with them. In return my colleague will spent her summer vacations in Supetar. And I was invited to Supetar. We had a great time in this beautiful summer ambient. Bit by bit Vanja and I become couple. We rented small apartment in Vienna we lived frugally, we studied and enjoyed our young lives. The wedding was next year in the summer in Zagreb. I was 24 and Vanja 21.

Vienna, 1973, D. Grünwald

JNA (Yugoslav army)

After I returned from Vienna to Zagreb 1968, I got a contract with Tvornica računskih strojeva TRS to redesign a small mechanical calculator. Around the time I completed this project I received an invitation from Yugo army to come for a physical exam to determine the army branch I should be put in. I was already married (27) and our daughter was two years old. I did not have any choice, I had to subjugate to their order. Vanja's father intervened by his colleagues which had high positions in the army to make sure that I will be placed close to Zagreb. It backfired! This intervention made them to send me to the furthest place, diagonal across Yugoslavia, to Strumica in Macedonia. It was known that this was the place for suspicious individuals.

The first three months I went through standard training. I was given a heavy gun to carry (20 kilograms). I felt like Jesus under the cross. Stronger soldiers offered to carry this monster for me. My captain called me "intellectual" and forced me, too often, to crawl in the dirt. I put up with that in cold blood since I knew that this Calvary will be over in a year.

My captain called me one day for discussion. He told me that the army does not recognize foreign universities therefore I have to serve a two years term! I was truly in shock! I tried nostrificate my diploma in Zagreb at University. They refused since there was no such program at this University. I finally got my nostrification at the Academy for applied arts in Belgrade and now I had to stay with the army one year only.

In my free time I went into the city (Strumica) and made sketches of interesting family houses. My captain noticed that and suggested I should organize art shop. Two fellow's soldiers, who completed Academy for applied art in Belgrade, joined me. We decided to create as much as possible artwork and mount an exhibit. I decided to experiment with oil paintings. My first work was a copy of Degas "Dancers". I was pleased with the results. My captain asked me to do his portrait. The portrait came out quite well, the captain could recognize himself! We created much of the artwork and organized the exhibit. All the soldiers went through the exhibit and they started to call me "Artist". Soon I become privileged soldier, I was allowed to go into the city and back whenever I wanted. I did not have to go to sudden exercise on the mountain in the middle of the night. I simply went to my art shop and continued sleeping. Officers, who lined up for their portraits, were protecting me of being disciplined. Only officers were allowed to use the swimming pool. I was the only one (from ordinary soldiers) who could swim any sunny day. I got the special assignment to guide parents of killed soldiers, through shopping spree. Greek or Bulgarian snipers were very active in the mountains.

I developed a good relationship with the local cultural center. I helped them by setting up their exhibits. They would invite me to their private celebrations, weddings, birthday parties, etc. If the event took place outside the city they would provide me with civil clothes. This way I got known well the Macedonians, very friendly, accessible characters.

The same people asked me to create something for the city carnival. I suggested making a two headed dragon. I constructed it from steel rods. It was huge monster not to heavy on four wheels. The only thing I forgot to check is the height of the electrical cables crossing the streets. The electricians had to remove these cables on the dragon's route.

A few weeks before my departure home high ranking officer, by the name Voljevac, asked me to make his portrait. I was already tired and was postponing his order. He realized that I am not going to do that so he reported to the general that I stole some paint. The general decided that Voljevac will search me before I will leave for home. I knew that this will be a trap and that Voljevac will plant something in my bag and this way frame me and I will end up in jail. One day before my departure, I got my walking papers. Next morning at 3 AM I sneak out through the hole in the fence and run to catch the first bus to Skoplje. In Skoplje I went straight to the airport and took the plane to Belgrade. I knew that Voljevac will send army police and they will search Strumica, trains and buses heading to Belgrade. I had Dinars for my plane ticket because I sold, two months ago, Walt Disney characters, in the size of small child, Miki, Mini, Pluto, Paja Duck to a local kindergarten.

A few days after I arrived in Zagreb one colleague whom I befriended in army, told me that Voljevac organized the hunt after me exactly the way I predicted. A few days later I was walking along the main street Ilica in Zagreb and suddenly I observed Voljevac walking toward me. He recognized me and turned sharply across the street. Most likely he was expelled from the army since he failed to search me. Nobody came after me since I had my official walking papers and Voljevac did not have any proof that I stole something. I was so glad that I outsmarted these army characters!

I made a portrait in the oil of Sergeant Luka Dzanko who rose to fame as a general in the Homeland War.

Silent exercise

This is a night exercise for soldieries when the moon is covered by the clouds. Captain had divided us in several small groups. We could communicate only by whispering. We were going through the thick forest in this dark night. Nothing you can see, we were nibbling the trees. I could not hear anyone and I suddenly become aware that I am all alone, lost in the forest. I decided to sit down and to wait until the morning. Now it becomes clear to me that I do not hear well. In Gymnasium and later at the University I always tried to sit up in front – to hear well! In the morning I found my way back.

At the first professional meeting of the Industrial Design Association we were sitting around a large oval desk. The colleague who was sitting diagonally (longer one) opposite of me had presentation. During the pause, he approached me and asked me what I think about his speech. I had to admit to him that I did not hear him - very embarrassing! The next day I went straight to an ear specialist. He explained to me that in my childhood the virus attacked my hearing center in the brain (electronics part). I remembered that I had often ear inflammations and my mother was treating me with hot oil. At that time antibiotics were not available. So in my 33 years of age, I got my first hearing aid. Doctor had mentioned that with the age I will be losing my hearing. He was right! Now in my 75 years of age in my right ear I have left only 5 % and in my left ear 25 % of hearing. Luckily my loss of hearing is being "followed" with every year better hearing aid technology. So I am still relatively OK!

Almost tragedy

This sunny, spring day in Toronto I was returning home from work, I turned around from the main street in my side road. I immediately noticed in second house block strong pulsating lights from the ambulance or police. I was coming closer to my house and both were standing in front of my house. I felt tingling, what is going on? I entered the house and found the scene, Vanja is lying on the couch in some kind of shock and the nurse was giving her the oxygen. The second nurse approached me and gave me explanation what has happened. Mladen was 4 ½ years old. Little Christina, the same age from the neighbors across the road, she came to play with Mladen. They were in the backyard and quite loud. Vanja noticed that they suddenly become silent. She went to look for them, but she could not find them. Now already in panic, she has gone through the garage, she tripped and she grabbed the handle of an old fridge and the door has opened. The kids fell out of fridge unconscious with freckles on their faces (sign of lack of oxygen) . She yelled from shock. Christina's mother heard this and came running over. Here are now my guesses since Vanja refused all these years to tell me some details. Most likely she does not now. I guess Christina's mother called emergency, brought the kids inside, most likely Vanja too. At the moment I entered the house the kids were already transferred to hospital. The second ambulance took me and Christina's mother to hospital. We did not wait too long, the doctor came and told us the good news, the kids did not suffer any damage. One day I took this old fridge out of my basement and placed in the garage and locked the door. I planed next day to remove fridge parts and place outside to be picked up. I was aware about the danger the old fridges represented since It was very often written in the newspaper about this kind of tragedies. My garage was locked. I assume that Vanja went into the garage and forgot to lock it. At the end it was my fault with Vanjas' "assistance". The next day there was an article about the event in the newspaper under my full name.

Summer downpour

"Cloudburst" is the other name for the enormous amount of rain in a short period of time. Mladen was six or seven years old. This rain created a "river" in our street which slightly descents toward the West. The warm rain water was almost up to Mladen's knees. We entertained ourself in front of the house next to the road. Mladen was maybe one meter next to me and he suddenly falls trough up to his neck. I grabbed him and pulled out without knowing what has just has happened. I noticed that on the spot I have pulled him out, the water created whirlpool and fast disappearing in some kind of hole. When the rain stopped I went to explore that hole. I had the explanation, I knew that long time ago small stream flow in this vicinity and that City put there large concrete tubes under the street. Most likely the tube broke during the harsh winter. Mladen stopped when he hits the concrete tube with his legs. I got the Goosebumps by the thoughts, if the hole would have been larger the water could have sucked Mladen in!

 I reported to the City and next day they repaired the damage.

Winter

The winter has pressed us this year heavily, -20. This kind of cold is not good for anything! Except, if your car starts under this condition that you know your battery is fine. My routine every morning is the same; I get up early at 6AM. At that time the emails from Europe usually have arrived (12 AM).

If I have to write some text this is the time while my mind is fresh. Lately I was working on interview with Mrs. Jasna Lovrinčević for her U VIHORU VREMENA, about my Life Time Achievement Award. This is already the third interview with her. I already translated all three texts in English which she will install in the English version of U VIHORU VREMENA. This WEB is well received around the word and being implemented in various Internet pages. So the Canadian Embassy presented these interviews in their pages.

Around 10 AM I usually go to YMCA Health Club and I spend there about 2 hours; I swim about 1 kilometer, I rest in a hot wire pool and massage myself with strong water jets. 15 minutes of steam bath cleanses my skin and fulfils my lung with hot, moist air. At the end I shave and take long shower. Now I am ready to go home and have a light lunch with my wife. I lie down for an hour – it feels good! In the afternoon I work with computer.

Plane ticket is in my pocket. I will arrive in Zagreb mid April. Until then, I will know, if Split's exhibit will be realized. I am very excited about that!

House

Previous days I completed all my written obligations, but today at 6 AM in the morning I have to write about something.

Our house is located in the geographic middle of Toronto. The "Spine" of the city is Yonge Street goes South-North. I was told that this street is the longest in the world, 43km. The highway "401" is going East-West. By this logic, I both small bungalow on the large lot 1980. , for Can $ 94000. Now a days the value of this property is around $2 000 000 ($ two millions). This was my best move in Canada. With the money I got from court case 1984., we enlarged and modernized the house. My son Mladen, when he was 16 (Now he is 41), built small apartment in the basement. He got married last year with nice girl Nancy. While we are in Croatia (6 months) the newlywed are taking care about the house.

Coffee

Since I returned from Zagreb I am going around Toronto visiting my old clients and trying to find the products I design 30 + years ago. I managed to get these way 5 products. They were shown at my first exhibit in Zagreb but only through the photographs.
In one company I got indication that their retired engineer got one such product (The one which received Canada Design Award). I got in touch with Đoko Mihailović (Serbian) and I went to visit him. I did not know what to expect and how he will treat me (Serbian – Croatian war 1990-1995!). He greeted me in a very cold manner and asked me what I need for this unit. I responded, for my exhibit in........in last moment I said Belgrade, instead Split. He responded, if this is so I am donating this to you. After that his wife served coffee and brandy (Slivovic).

Children

My daughter Andrea (50) lives in small city Keswick, North of Toronto. From door to door is 60 km and it takes me 40 minutes highway drive. They are facing Lake Simco and have a huge ship tied up in their backyard. They have two sons; Gabriel (20) is from Andrea's first marriage and Kyle (14) from now second.

With her first husband Andrea went through calvary, he was Canadian Kickboxing Champion but he succumbed to drugs and alcohol. While ago, he died (53) from the aftermath of his troubled life.

Andrea is a dental hygienist. In Zagreb this professional profile has not been established yet. Dentists are performing this task. Andrea is now Reborn, she has near perfect marriage and her new husband is totally opposite of the first one. Andrea is similar to me; patient, not hesitant, chooses carefully her options, and makes rational decisions. She is very successful in her job, everybody loves her and appreciates.

Andrea's drawing, 8

Mladen's drawing, 8 (on the old fens)

My son Mladen (42) is now in heaven! He is in the first year of marriage. He is a manager in large real estate office (industrial building, warehouses, office buildings etc.). He is multi talented, creative individual. Every year when we return from Croatia something large has been done to the house; replacing old windows, new roof shingles etc.

We enjoy our kids enormously!

Wife, Vanja

Vanja, graduated from the Applied Art School, interior in Zagreb. There was no work for her in Yugoslavia. In Canada, she specialized in kitchen design for ten years. She was then preoccupied with ceramics, so she created objects based on my Sculptra; vases, ashtrays, wall compositions. In recent years, she's indulged in abstract explorations.

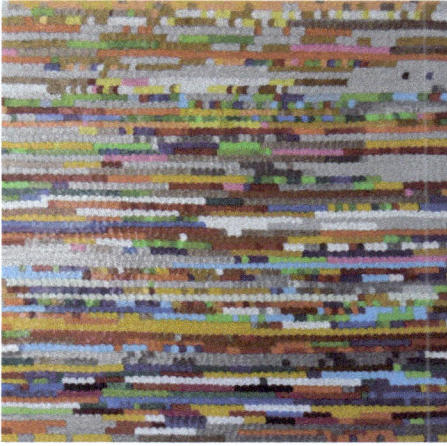 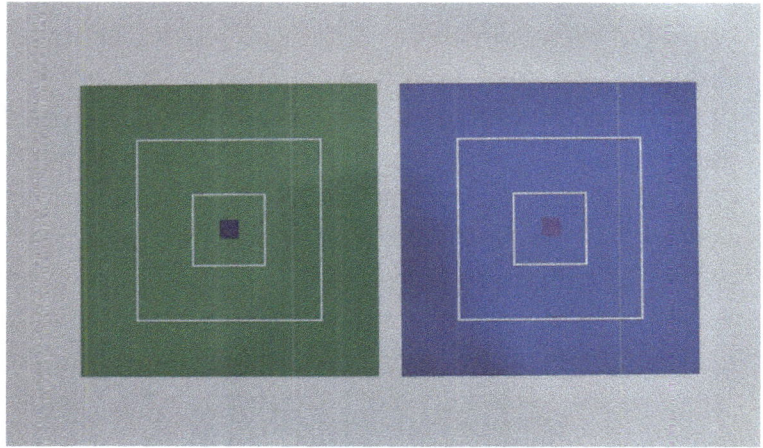

KrK

Five years ago I bought a small flat in Draga Bascanska, 3 kilometers before Baska on island Krk. The flat is in 100 years old building, renovated with water, electricity and canalization. I bought this so my family at large could have some vacation. None of them managed to buy something on Adriatic's. It is only 200 km from Zagreb.

I usually come to Croatia mid April, one month earlier than my wife. I go to Krk to prepare the flat for the new summer season. With the local hiking club I spend some time on beautiful mountains enjoying fresh, exotic air and breathtaking views. On the way to island Brač (Split) we usually stay a few days on Krk. In high season Krk is full of tourist, so we avoid Krk at that time.

My flat is located at the end of narrow cu-de-sac outside of any crowd. If I wish to plunge into the ocean I take my bicycle and in 15 minutes I am there. Going to Baška it is downhill, but going back.....that's why I bought my electric bike, definitely a good solution for older persons.

Garage

While we were working in Canada, we could have only one month vacation in Croatia. Since we got retired we, stay in Croatia six months. We land in Zagreb and stay approximately one week to see our family. We used one apartment while in Zagreb. A few years ago this apartment was not available any more. I brought an expensive car from Canada, Porsche Boxster, which could not stay on the street or backyard. I bought a large garage (50 m2) in Trokut (across the river Sava) and from the half I build a living space. The other half remained garage for two cars. This is a great solution for our circumstances; the car is protected for six months and we can stay in Zagreb as long as we wish without bothering anyone. We are enjoying the ride on great roads in Croatia visiting places we failed to see while being in Canada. The friends are telling me, one another of yours design solutions.

Operations

They were few! But they could be characterized as a classic. The first was in my forties, right hernia. In Toronto there is a world renowned private hospital for hernias only, Shouldice Hernia Hospital. The patients are coming from all over the world. Ten years later I got operated my left hernia in the same hospital.

Sometimes around that time I got "Fistula in ano". This is fistula, which feeds itself from the guts. It blossoms in approximately every two months and then burst. I was joking that I menstruate. The first doctor told me there is no help; I have to live with that. I "lived with that" for ten years and then I found another doctor who agreed to operate. The fistula came back! I decided to find the doctor with a good reputation for this kind of problem. I run into the best one in North America in one Toronto hospital. I was waiting for a year for my first appointment and the other six months for operation term. It was all worth, the fistula never came back. This doctor proofed his reputation. From this experience I would recommend to consult at least three doctors for one medical problem. With this I lived for 15 years.

It is known that the man's start getting prostate problems in their fifties. I was right on dot; I got the diagnosis of enlarged prostate. If I consumed coffee or any drink with tannin my "pipe" would be squished. I had to run to the hospital to get the catheter. My friends in Supetar recommended young doctor, specialist for laser operations (no knife cutting) already with great reputation. I will never forget his name, Dr. Šitum. Partial removal of the prostate is being done through the "pipe". Prostate cannot now squish the "pipe". Test of the prostate sample did not show any cancer. Now I can enjoy in coffee and red wine. With this all my medical troubles disappeared and I can enjoy fully my retiring days. Based on this experience I would recommend visiting three doctors for one medical problem.

Gabriel

My older grandson Gabriel is studying English. Very early he started to express himself with drawings. He would always surprise us with content, composition, details. I concluded that he is very advanced for his age. Now his art reached maturity of an accomplished artist. I asked my colleague Vlado Kuharić, Academic, painter, about his opinion about Gabriel's art. He said that Gabriel is a "Young Bosch". He was accepted at Art Academia but he chooses English since he enjoys literature as well. Professors at University noticed him since he illustrates his essays.

18 of age

22 of age

Professor Patricia Počanić: A real artistic family! Very imaginative and interesting drawings and graphics, there really is something of Bosch in it. I think it's also a great combination of colleges for computer animation and English and literature (it's a very vibrant area of art). I find it particularly interesting the influence comics, sci-fi and fantasy literature, culture and visuals.

What a character!

(About Marijan Oresić, ex professor at School of Design)

This Sunday I met my younger colleagues, he just graduated Industrial Design four years after me. I commented to him that next day at 2 PM I have an appointment in Jadran, factory of tubular furniture, for the position of R&D Director. As soon I came in, the President asked me, who is the young fellow, Marijan Oresić who came in at 6 AM and offered himself for position of Director of R&D? I could not believe that my friend whom I helped a lot in Vienna, we even shared a rented room and I was his godfather at his wedding, that he could do such thing! I am more disgusted with the fact that when he arrived in his mature age he never felt the need to apologise for this behavior when he was a youngster. I got this well paid position. Three months later the President called me for discussion and told me that now since I am in leading position I have to join the communist party. My answer was "No thanks" and I turned around and left the company for good.

Smart

After the swimming in the YMCA I sometimes visit our friends B. and M. who live nearby. We discussed my past in Croatia. I was R&D director of Jadran factory. The director ordered me to join the communist party. I responded "No thanks" and left the company instantly. (Described in "What a character"). B. commented that the smart people would accept such an offer. I responded that I call such people "Opportunists". Applied to me B. indirectly said I was stupid and all the Croats who left Croatia because of the communist regime. I did not want to discuss any more on that subject and I left. His wife was present! I came home and wrote an email:
"B. if someone would join communists not being convinced in their cause, but from greed, then I would call this: hypocrisy, low behaviour without pride and consistency, opportunism. These people are saying now that it was better living in Yugoslavia.
If you call this SMART, then I have doubt in your good personal character".

Friend

(about Dinko Zlatarić, Architect and painter-portraitist)

D. was my great friend from the grade one until a few years ago. We experienced together many adventures typical for the age we went through. In Rugvice, a small village near Zagreb, his family owned old house and some field property. In river Sava we found a large fish in the box. We brought the fish to D's mom saying, we caught it. She prepared fine fish lunch. While we were sitting around the table the bell rang. It was a villager whose fish we just ate!

D. graduated as an architect and then went to Germany and studied art –painting. He specialized in portraits and was accepted in the World portraits club. Every time I came to Croatia I visited him and his wife Vera. During the last getting together, I told them in details about manic depression of one member of my family. As of then he never responded to my emails or telephone calls.

D's mother was a very fine lady, but in older age she started to behave insane, scene after scene. She had severe case of manic depression.   Once I was present at such episode. D's father was a Head of Law University, wel known and famous. He did not endure, left the family. I am guessing that my story remained D. of this difficult period of life and he just cracked!

Friendship cannot be taken lightly and for granted. It has to be treated with honesty, respect and attention. DG

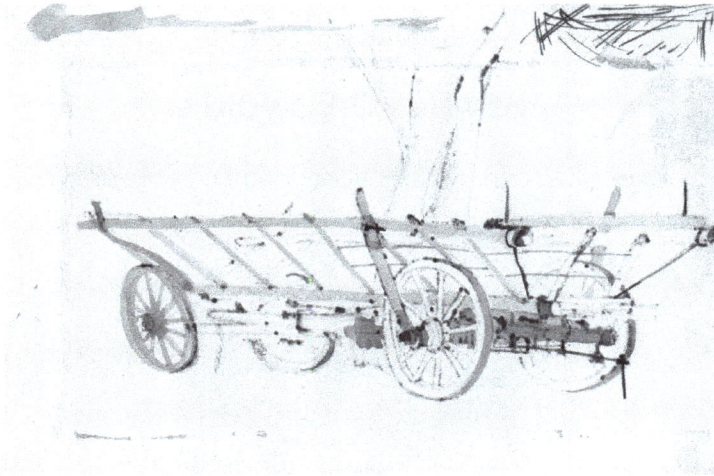

Burgendland, Austria, 1964, D. Grünwald

Necked island (Goli otok), prison

Vanja's father was very a pleasant conversationalist. You could tell that he went through many ordeals in his life. He was illegal conspirator, part of the secret communist party during the Second World War. He was an idealist, but very honest. His secret name was "Varja". After the war he had some role in the justice system. He refused to carry on one illegal order "From above". He was snapped on the street and shipped to Goli otok (prison). Vanja's mother did not know for a year where her husband disappeared. The father managed to smuggle a short note, I am on Goli otok, I do not know when (if) I will be back. The life under most inhumane condition forced him three times to try to kill himself. He was one of the lucky once; he was released after two years.

He got a job in Geophysical Company and his boss was Savka Dapčević Kučar (Croatian Spring movement around seventies). He managed from two small salaries (Vanja's mother was a teacher) to build a cottage in Supetar (Island Brač. By working hard he saved himself from the psychological burden from the war and Goli otok.

When the Serbian aggression started against Croatia, Vanja's parents were our guests in Toronto. Nobody could stop the father; he returned to Zagreb and insisted to be accepted in the Croatian army. He was too old and the army rejected him.

Already in old age (84) he worked hard on a very hot day and got dehydrated. The emergency fast boat took him to Split's hospital. During the night hospital stuff forgot about him and he died on the corridor. At that time the hospital was full of injured soldiers (war with Serbs!)

A few years ago Vanja and I went to visit Goli otok. Now this is a tourist destination. It surprised us how much garbage in these dilapidated buildings there was. I sent an email to Mr. Josipović, shame! The next day I got the responds that he has sent my email to the appropriate department. Later on I learned that his father was the head of all prisons in Yugoslavia (including the one on Goli otok).

Famous Grünwald's

With me on the same page of Croatia's Bibliographic Encyclopedic are my grandfather Josip and uncle Dražen and Branko.

Prof. Ing. Josip Grünwald

Grandpa Josip Grunwald, 1881. – 198

My grandfather, Josip Grünwald, is one of the founders of the Faculty of Forestry in Zagreb. He was a professor at that college. In his lectures he spoke that Medvednica (Sljeme) is ZAGREB 's lungs and that therefore it should be declared PROTECTIVE FORESTS . In 1981 Medvednica was declared a NATURE PROTECTION PARK. He took care of count Pejačević's possessions in Našice. He bought from him a large property on the slopes below mount Papuk, in Seona (a small village near Naice) and built a large oak two-storey house and all the outbuildings. He cultivated and studied fruit trees and vines. He shared the results of his work with the villagers and helped them. Now at the Pejačević Castle in Našice Museum, grandpa is prominently displayed. Here are a few anecdotes about him:

1936. Josephine Becker came to Zagreb. My grandfather and a friend got into a carriage and dragged Josephine trough Zagreb.

He went with his two wheel carriage to celebrate with the villagers. He came home usually drunk and he'd fall asleep. The horse knew the way to Seona.

When the Communists took a large part of his land in Seona, in 1946, he cut the vireyard with an ax and was no longer himself.

I was 5 years old. He ordered me to hold two donkeys by the reins. Donkeys went each to their sides, stretched me out, I let them go! I hid in the hay with fear of my grandfather. They were calling me out, looking all over the place. I got out of my hideout around the suppertime.

Uncle Dražen Grünwald was an actor, director at Gavela and professor at the Accdemia. In the theatre I was always sitting in the first row.

Uncle Branko Grünwald was a pathology doctor. He was ordered by communist to dissect Alojs Stepinac when he was killed by the m.

Prof. Ing. Mladen Grünwald

Father Mladen Grünwald, 12913. – 1944.

PUBLISHED IN ECONOMIC MESSENGER, JANUARY 1944, ZAGREB

In the extraordinary circumstances in which we live, both the scariest and most difficult events, which we could not have imagined before, as if they now do not surprise any of us and as if we have learned to consider them normal. So at first glance, but still the unused horrific, tragic death of Ing. Mladen Grünwald, teacher of the State Secondary School of Economics in Križevci, reflected the dismay and sincere sadness on the faces of everyone, rot just his friends and companions, not just those with who Ing. Grünwald cooperated, not only those who knew him more closely, but also those who had heard of him, because they only heard good about him. There was great sadness for the young economic expert, from whom was much expected. Quiet, calm, settled, master of himself, and hard-working, and self-professed economic expert, Ing. Grünwald went silent by accident, leaving behind an inconsolable wife and two innocent children and old, good parents, for whom they were pride.

Ing. Grünwald was born in Djakovo in 1913. After finishing high school in Zagreb, he enrolled at the Faculty of Agriculture and Forestry in Zagreb, and finished it in 1937. He earned his love for agronomic studies in his home. That's where love was inherited from the father and he and his younger brother, because they both devoted themselves to agriculture science. The idealist above all dedicated himself to the most ideal and noble industry, fruiting. The first service of every expert, especially an economic expert, is often crucial for his professional development and for the future direction of his work. The hardest hits are the wandering. Ing. Grünwald didn't wander. He was lucky when, in 1939, he was appointed to the State High School of Economics. The old, renowned school has provided a young expert with all the possibilities for his improvement in the selected branch. Lately - and extraordinary opportunities dictated this, his interest has grown increasingly in the processing of fruits and vegetables. In connection with the plan of the Ministry of The Peasant Economy in the issue of the production of fruit and garden products for the nutrition of the population, Ing Grünwald was sent to Germany. He worked for three months at Stendel's fruit and vegetable processing plant. There, he is personally involved in all processing. He himself does all the processing work himself, in order to transfer his experience to his homeland and to be as capable as he can in organizing similar institutions with us in Croatia. In this regard, immediately after his return to his homeland, he worked around the organization of processing at the School of Economics in Križevci, in order to then expand his activity further into the surrounding areas. But fate wanted that work, imbued with idealism, to be tragically interrupted by his death on May 7th. 1944. His magnificent funeral in Zagreb, where his earthly remains were laid to eternal rest, is a testament to the great corporeity and deep pain of all who accompanied him for the last time. Therefore, may his glory and lasting memory be in our hearts.

Dr. F. Pasković

About Željko Borčić (1942–2015)

He was a very successful and respected graphic designer. We knew each other for the last ten years. I read his biography somewhere and spotted his Canadian episode. I came to Croatia every year and it was "mandatory" for me to go to Samobor where we (my family) had a weekend house on Anindol (below the restaurant). I visited Željko routinely every time and he and his wife were always invited to our weekend house when we had some festivities. I was surprised to be told that his wife was an American-born, she spoke fluent Croatian. Željko would sometimes take me to the small restaurants, which served local specialties, on the slopes of the hill above Samobor where we spent hours discussing our professional experiences. He was a pleasant interlocutor (but an unpleasant smoker - a cigarette after a cigarette!). The last time I visited him the sickness already was crushing him. I'm glad I knew him, and I'm so sorry that he left us too soon.

No time
(About Anton Cetin, the famous world wide abstract painter)

With A. C. I was friend for more than thirty years. He is great artist and is one of the few making good money with his art. He is known to be an excelled businessman. He has very often exhibits in Croatia. His paintings are abstract but understandable for ordinary viewer. He is known for his famous topic "Eve and the bird". We helped each other whenever there was a need for help. I often visited him just to comment on his new artwork. We visited each other with our wife's, having lunch and suppers. He and his family were guests at our house in Supetar. I was witnessing the signature of his 102 year old mother. I never refused his request for help.
I was preparing materials for my exhibit in Zagreb. I needed a good text about my spherical shape Sculptra. He got a Sculptra composition as a gift and he always commented with high regards about this shape. I asked him to write a text about Sculptra since he writes well and has a vocabulary for such task. He responded with short email: "I have no time" ! There was no additional explanation like, in a week, month etc. I got really hurt with such response. I wrote him back: "I do not have time for you as well"
The matter stayed on this note!

Accent

In the newspaper I found an add that the School for Applied Art "Emily Car" in Vancouver is looking for an Industrial design professor. They invited me for an interview. I spent three days in this beautiful city. I met five professors and presented my portfolio. At the end, the dean told me that I was accepted in the first round and they will inform me about the details by mail. The letter came one month later. I had to lose my accent in a year! I responded that I noticed that all persons, I spoke too, had an accent – British! Most likely I will never lose my accent. Of course I did not get the job.

Lady Diana

In 1997. in Toronto there was held the world industrial design congress (ICSID). I was personally very engaged in the event; I organized the exhibit of Canadian Industrial Designers. For this occasion I collected slides presentation from my colleagues, including my own, for example; land mine detector. At that time Lady Diane was very active trying to prevent the production of land mines. I sent her a letter on June 1, 1997. asking for her support. She sent me a letter of support on June 17. In 1997, I read during my presentation and I got public applause. Unfortunately, on August 30, 1997. she lost tragically her life. Her letter has great value.

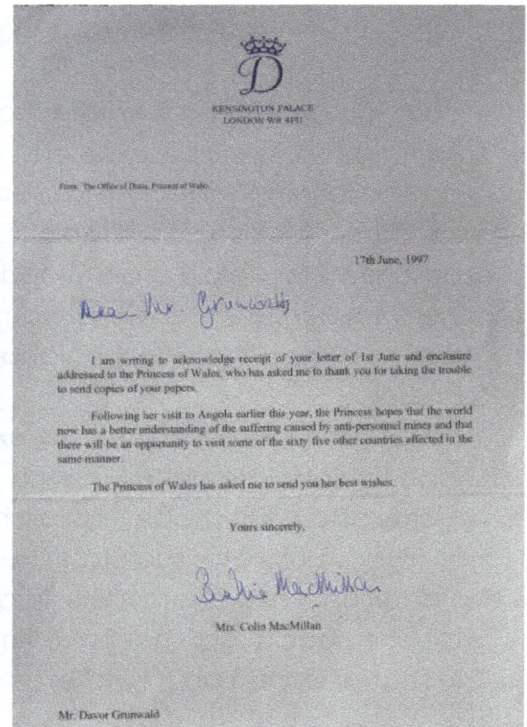

Lady Diana's letter

What behavior!

During the war (1990-1995) in the Balkans I traveled to Zagreb several times and gave lectures and seminars at the School of Design in Zagreb. On one occasion, I met Mr. Ivan Dorogy then president of ULUPUH, the Association of Applied Arts, in Zagreb who asked me to send him my materials and designs created in Europe, the US and Canada. I sent him a package with twelve panels (20" x 30"), ready to be exhibited. A few days after the arrival of my package in ULUPUH, the Party of Rights (Stranka prava), a political party, occupied the building by weapon force, where ULUPUH had its offices. They kicked out the tenants and tossed their furniture and documents into the basement. My wife arrived from Canada a few days later and immediately went to try to save my materials. There was an armed, bearded man at the door. Inside the building, some men greeted her with Hitler's salute. She managed to get permission to inspect the basement (under the watchful eye of an armed soldier). She found nothing. I had lost my exhibition materials, but fortunately I had sent copies of the original panels that I had used for presentations in Canada. Mr. Dorogy never contacted me again after this incident.

Business drama

In 1980 I got a job in Toronto with Delphax Ltd., Ion deposition fast printers. After 3 years about ten of us were offered to move to Boston. I accepted, but I did not want to relocate my family in haste. They agreed to pay me a return ticket to Toronto once a month. Problems arose three months later when the company decided to give the development contract to a Japanese company (including industrial design). I became surplus labor. Then the provocations began from my American boss, the deputy chairman. He summoned us all to the meeting room. The first item on the agenda was a question directed at me. "Davor, tell us, why did you design our new logo in red? Didn't you know that the traditional American colour is blue?" Rather than explaining to them the actual visual and graphic reasons for my choice, I responded, "Mr. Mastedino, have you forgotten that the company is still Canadian, and the Canadian traditional colour is red, just look at the Canadian flag!" My boss first blanched, then turned red (not blue!) in the face and rushed out of the room. I knew he was actually provoked me and implying that because I had come from communist Yugoslavia, I was using the color red to promote communism on American soil. I knew that I had defended the Canadian colors and flag. It cost me my well-paid job, but I never regretted it.

The next morning, my boss was waiting for me and pointed toward the exit. I was told to pack my personal belongings within an hour to report the next day to human resources management in Toronto. The lady in Toronto, who was responsible for personnel, was waiting for me. She said that I had quit verbally in Boston and that according to my contract I must return all the money that they had invested in me. I told her that this was a lie. I had been fired and according to the contract, I did not owe them anything. I announced to her that I planned to sue the company for wrongful dismissal. She said that if I did that I would never get another job in Canada. Companies usually seek information from former employers. The last thing I told her was, "Watch me!"

I hired the best employment lawyer in Canada, Howard Levitt, who specialized in wrongful dismissal cases. Canadian labor laws were created based on Mr. Howard Levitt's cases. After two years of litigation, I won the case and a large settlement. I was told that if the case had been tried in America, I would not have had a chance. Mr. Mastedino, my former boss, was ousted from the company. I later learned that he was a CIA intelligence officer. After this experience, I realized that I had no interest in American arrogance and that I would concentrate on Canada only. I built an addition to the house with the settlement money and lived for two years with no income. The personnel lady badmouthed me to potential employers in the worst possible way and I could not get a job for two years.

Floods

One night I was descending the stairs into the basement part of the house. I didn't turn on the light. All of a sudden I feel cold water, almost knee-deep. Nothing can prepare you for that kind of shock. There's a thought going through my brain, it's raining all day, it's been leaking somewhere! I'm calling 911 right now for help. Firefighters arrive quickly and begin pumping water. The city inspector comes in and stops this activity with an explanation: On the sides of the road there is sewage for rainwater and in the middle of the road there is a sewer for dirty water: toilet, kitchen, and bathroom. The filthy water manhole in front of our house was plugged and the water, going after least resistance, entered to our basement. The city team came, the manhole was unplugged and the water receded from our basement, but it left a big mess. By order of the inspectors, we were not allowed to touch anything because it was brown, the toilet water from all the houses in front of us. The next day, insurance sent a team of people to fix the mess. First, they threw all the furniture and stuff soaked in that contaminated water in the trash. All the wall surfaces, one meter from the floor, and the floors also ended up in the trash. The wall structures were washed with lime for disinfection. The walls and floor were restored with new materials. That lasted a month. The insurance bill was $40,000! This covered the cost of new furniture and belongings as well. In the short time after that, I hired a company that installs a valve that does not allow passage of dirty water into the house. The city incurred half the cost. It's been six years without such new problems. We returned in the autumn from Croatia and find the whole basement differently arranged than when we left for Croatia in the spring. We asked Mladen, our son, for an explanation: He said, again, it was identical flood, but now the valve remained open because some hard object prevented it from closing and the contaminated water entered the basement area. Mladen did not want to spoil our stay in Croatia, so he did everything in his arrangement without informing us! He also installed a pump in the basement that automatically dumps water out on the road. Since then, the city is often controlling our manhole and others. A third flood would be really too much for one life.

$ 100 000

In 1984. I landed a freelance job with Geonics, geophysical company. The Vice-president was my track and field colleague from Zagreb. They developed EM38 electromagnetic device to check the farm field quality before planting the new seeds. It was really ugly looking thing, with components scattered all over the wooden frame. I organize components for easy production and maintenance, added ergonomic features for easy handling and gave aesthetical value to the product. After this very successful intervention the President has offered me permanent job which I accepted. After four times, redesigning / improving EM38 (mostly electronics) in the span of 34 years, it remained very much the same looking device.

I was with Geonics 24 years and designed all products Geonics is selling nowadays (approximately 20). I was part of R&D together with the President and few electronic engineers. Production was handled by the fellow technician from Split, Croatia. I never met anyone with such huge envy and jealousy. He used every opportunity to attack me, badmouth me behind my back. Numerous time I was forced to report this to the President in writing and verbally. There was no change in his behavior. My last year (2015) he added a "New" method to harass me, he called me names in front of workers, like; old shit head, old fart etc. Again the President did nothing to rectify the situation. I hired the lawyer, gave him ten pages of documents I collected within 24 years with Geonics. The lawyer wrote two pages letter to the President stating that if this will continue Davor will sue Geonics, President and technician (in the meantime, he got the title Vice-President of Production) for human rights and harassment. The President fired me and offered me $ 100 000 not to sue them. I accepted!

Interesting, in my life span I had quite a few disagreements and court cases. I won all and collected this way quite a bit of money.

AMCA

IN TORONTO, ASSOCIATION
OF EX ALUMNI AND FRIENDS
OF UNIVERSITIES IN
REPUBLIC OF CROATIA

U TORONTU, DRUSTVO
BIVSIH STUDENATA I
PRIJATELJA SVEUCILISTA
U REPUBLICI HRVATSKOJ

Proposal for a new letterhead AMCA

Professor šeparovic from the University of Zagreb initiated 1989 branch associations in every major city in the world of ex students of Croatian Universities under the title: ALMA MATRIS CROATICA ALUMNI (AMCA). Our branch in Toronto started with 100 members, but soon swelled to 300. At the very beginning we (Board of Directors) decided to publish every two month's magazine by the name GAUDEAMUS in English. This was our platform to present the latest news, actual happenings in politics, culture and history and other newsworthy information's. Contributions had arrived from the other branches as well. This was a very dynamic activity, but demanded lots of energy and time. I was 10 years the Vice-president of AMCA-Toronto and was responsible for visual aspects and production of Gaudeamus. I designed the cover by using a large University of Zagreb emblem.

University of Zagreb emblem

During the last war with Serbians (1990 – 1995) Gaudeamus plaid a large role in informing Canadian Parliamentarians about the truth aspects of this imposed war, Serbian aggression. This was the only opposition to Serbian official propaganda machinery delivered through Yugoslav Embassy. A significant factor in the Canadian attitude (accepting the Serbian lies) towards this war was Brian Malruni's (Canadian Prime Minister at that time) wife Mila, of Serbian decent. We published many frightening photographs about Serbian rampages (Vukovar, Srebrenica, Dubrovnik and many others). We organized gala suppers and the profits have been sent to these distressed cities for their renewal. A few years ago I visited these city's and one could not tell that they were once destroyed. Here I have to underline that this was the most important role of this first AMCA Board of Directors. The Board of Directors/Presidents which have followed, they never acknowledged the fact that we played that significant historical role during the last war. Fortunately, the activities of the first Management Board (1990–2000) were presented by President I. Hrvoić and Vice President V.

Benković, through all documentation from this period, in two thick volumes that are stored in the Croatian National Library, "for ever and ever" – BRAVO! The current President K. Mustapić has publicly attacked them for this – SHAME! ! The same way, the Board of Directors, which followed, they never invited me to hold a presentation about Industrial Design, even after I received the Life Achievement Award and very successful exhibits in Zagreb and Split. Animosity towards the first Board of Directors is present in many forms, so most likely it has been "transferred" towards me as well.

 I suggested a new trade mark (on the right) to replace the one (on the left) which is totally inacceptable – judged by the standard graphic design criteria. The author of that sign, Nada Raffay, I gave detailed explanation of why I think so.

Old & new trademarks, AMCA

New AMCA Board of Directors rejected my proposal without explanation! One more behavior of people without "Kinderstube". In an email exchange, the AMCA president, Krešo Mustapić, called me "Sujetan". It's the Serbian word for "Pretentious". I replied that that description fits him far better. I dropped out of this kind of AMCA !

My "NOW" from being retired 2008 until now

 I retired in my 68 years of age. While than I was able to stay only 30 days in a year in Croatia and now as retiree I can stay – six months. My basis is in Supetar on island Brač where we have a house. From there, with my spouse, we travel, explore the beautiful ours (Croatia). In Zagreb we stay a short time, only passing through. I did not stop designing. But now I do not have to deal with corporate nonsense and fighting with coworkers. I design objects for which I consider to be valuable to invest some energy. This is now more or less my hobby. On island Brač I am surrounded by natural beauties which support my creative inspiration and in Toronto or Zagreb I am producing the prototypes.

A good example is the Elips chair. I was curious if I am capable of designing a chair that should be different than "small million chairs" by using CNC production technology, without any tooling investment and with minimal materials. I called this minimalist approach. Now, after three prototypes I can state that I succeeded in fulfilling these self-given criteria The Porsche Boxster rack was inspired by my personal need. I enjoy driving this car for the last ten years. But when I travel with my spouse the rack comes handy to mount a large suitcase. I offered this rack to my colleagues, Boxster owners in North America and I sold quite a few. Even in Zagreb I sold one on the street!

Elips chair and Porsche rack

Impressions of the state of industrial design in Croatia

I have certain impressions about the condition of industrial design in Croatia, All factories, for which I worked at the beginning of seventies last century, do not exist any more. After proclaiming the Croatian Republic, Tudman gave these factories, after the pronouncement of Croatian republic, to be managed, by his political followers. They failed to invest in R&D and the products could not compete with Western technologies so these factories closed the doors for good. Of course the war was raging in the Balkans (1990-1995). Now there are many small private companies with high production technologies which are producing highly sophisticated parts for foreign clientele. These companies do not need industrial designers.

Of course, there are a few exceptions: Rimac electric cars, Ericson/Tesla products. In genera, there are very few companies with originally developed and designed products. What are all these graduated industrial designers going to do? Small numbers of those manage to get a contract with some foreign companies. Others are designing the wood products and trying to sell the ideas.

Strong industrial base is needed for industrial design to exist. Croatia lost its industrial base, therefore has not the potential for industricl design to grove. The efforts trough government institutions to educate the public about Industrial design are just coquetting with the idea. Croatia becomes the service country for developed ones. Croatia will further export the highly educated professionals including industrial designers. Abroad they are achieving above average results. How come? Because in these countries the innovation and new development is being stimulated.

Therefore I am suggesting to Croatian Government to stimulate to maximum the companies which have developed their products and are hiring industrial designers and helped them to export abroad. They should also develop programs for companies which have the technological capacity to develop their own products with the help of industrial designers. This is a way how the Croatian industrial base will recover and industrial designers will find jobs. This should be part of Croatian economic growth.

I am returning to Croatia every year and staying six summer months not to act as incustrial designer but to enjoy the scenery in Croatia which I did not experience while living and working in Canada.

By archiving my professional opus in MUO, exhibits in Zagreb and Split and receiving the Live Achieving Award are valuable recognitions for my professional efforts the last 50years.

2CV

The "ugly duckling" is the name of a popular French car, the Citroen 2CV. They started production in 1948. and since then it conquered the world with its unconventional characteristics and look. Citroen 2CV was produced for 41 years until 1989.

 I decided to travel from island Brač to Samobor for the 23rd world meeting of the 2CV, in 2019 took place. It was announced that over 3000 2CVs will be present for the event, from all over the world. They came 5000 strong!

Behind the Samobor's bus terminal there is a huge grass field. All 2CV and their owners with their tents settled there. The people asked me why I decided to see this colossal spectacle? Many did not know that I as a student in Vienna (1964 - 1968) bought a yellow, ten yeasr old 2CV which had 14 HP. I traveled often between Vienna and Zagreb (400 km) to get food supply for the next period. In the winter, the roads were covered by snow and I could not climb a steep road portion, so I turned 2CV backwards and drove in reverse, to gain traction.

Our daughter Andrea (now 51) "grew up' in the 2CV. As soon as she was born, she was laying in a crib on the rear bench. When she grew stronger, she would jump on the 2CV's bumper, and enjoyed its famous rear springs - swinging 2CV. The 2CV was a superb car for the Brač gravel roads.

I sold my yellow 2CV to my colleague, who weighed over 100 kg. During driving over the road "bump", the chassis broke in half. Hi disassembled the car and welded two strong steel profiles - now the 2CV was fit to carry his weight.

I bought a new TOMOS 2CV and enjoyed the ride until my departure to Canada 1975 2CV is famous for its practicality. Once I transported a bed - the most of it sticks through the open roof. From the moment I bought this yellow 2CV I knew that this kind of car could only be created by a genius. It was one of my favorite examples how to approach design concepts. This served me well through my 50 years of practice as an industrial designer.

I had to experience the enthusiasm and creativity of 2CV owners, who participated in the 23rd world meeting. To some I offered my Porsche Boxster 2006 in exchange for their 2CV. I got loud NO from everyone!

The original intention of the Citroen 1948 was to offer to French farmers economical transportation of their produce from the field. Citroen did not anticipate that this car will become the world phenomenon for its universality, the symbol of simplicity and multiple practicalities. I am glad that I was one of many who recognized these facts.

Volkswagen's BUG become popular as well. But VW decided to take advantage of this phenomenon and come up with NEW BUG and made a tremendous financial success. The same has happened with the Fiat 500. I hope that Citroen will follow the suit one day.

.....and the winner is: the red 2CV - with restoration, which maintained the integrity of the original 2CV in all details. The owner exchanged the wheels for "wired" once and "redesigned" the rear wheel covers which suits 2CV very well and he added well designed trailer for additional things.

Croatian Telekom

I have an interesting case with Croatian Telecom: I last used the Internet in Croatia during an exhibition in TMNT - November 2019. Before leaving for Toronto I went to the branch H. T. and requested stillness. Their employee assured me that I didn't need any documentation from them. H. T. sent me an invoice (100 K) every month and I didn't "twitch" so they send me a warning that I had to pay them until the end of my contract, June 2020. I objected to them that I am standing by my story, and that they could sue me. But because their employee tricked me, I wouldn't want to deal with them. A solution has come from their head of objections: They checked; stillness has not been established, I have not had any activity since December 2019. and therefore they have accepted my explanation and they no longer have any claims. I thanked the head of objections and promised that when I came to Croatia I would continue with them because they proved that they were fair. I talked to my younger sister about it and she said I'm a lucky and foxy. I replied that I don't accept either. "Luck" I build myself and people who are decent to me, I return double. To those who insult me, I give them double back. I took that off my principles list.

Everyday's dynamic

Grünwald family honors distancing during Coronavirus crisis, 2020, Daughter Andrea, grandson Kyle, Davor, wife Vanja. son Mladen, daughter-in-law Nancy

CORONAVIRUS has ruled the world, people are dying, and there is no vaccine! As I recall, my parents' generation was faced with THE SPANISH FLU AND TUBERCULOSIS, and until the vaccines were found - millions of people died! At the time of my childhood POLIO and more recently SARS and AIDS were prevented by vaccine. And this time it will take at least one year to find the vaccine for the Corona virus to be suppressed.

My daily dynamic, under these circumstances (and all the people in the world), is greatly disrupted. My wife and I are "hiding" in our house because we belong to the most dangerous group over 70. Our son brings us groceries and we very rarely go to get something with a high dose of caution. Instead of daily swimming, I go for long walks in our neighborhood - there are no people. We cancelled our trip to Croatia (in May 2020) and booked a plane ticket for May 2021 (just so we could use the money paid).

Our son Mladen and his wife Nancy were visiting her parents in China when the Corona virus crisis erupted in China. They caught the last plane to Toronto and were in isolation for 14 days. At this time of forced isolation, I am preoccupied with working on my Great Monograph. This activity saves me! It will be a book of about 300 pages (with English translation). Definitely, the comments of my friends are INSPIRATION/MOTIVATION FOR THIS BOOK. Here are a few examples:

You thrilled me to the immense pleasures of watching your exhibition, I knew there was a self-contained "devil-sage" in you, but not to the extent that I've now figured it out. I congratulate you on all your feats and successes, and I want your life to continue to be exciting and beautiful, well done, I'm so happy for your happiness, your satisfaction after all the effort and everything you've had to deal with in years past, but the justice and modesty you've been boasting have done their part. I congratulate you with all my heart and I want you to enjoy the well-deserved "glory". A big kiss from me! Well done, hooray!
  Dr. Jaja Tomašković, Zane

This exhibition is the most complete presentation of all that has been presented so far by this talented and extremely successful designer from our premises. A beautiful picture of the development path, which also shows that in addition to talent and will, persistent work is often required with thorny obstacles. Your story should be published to our young people as a roadmap in today's world of deranged values in which it is not popular to create and work, which is however the only true path to progress. Congratulations!
Zvonko Kuharić, Dipl. Ing.

I am delighted to have been present at significant events related to your work and thus had the opportunity to know your life path and professional achievements. This third, comprehensive exhibition at TMNT, could certainly be stimulating for young people, especially in these our areas. If everyone were so responsibly, boldly and diligently developing their talents, from God, the world would look different.
Palma Orlović-Leko, PhD

This is an exhibition (TMNT, 26 Sudeni '19 – 1 February '20) to which one should take himself, children, grandchildren, or younger relatives, and remember some days when this country could give some essential work experience and other professions than medical ones, before going belly-after bread to some distant countries in search of a fairer salary for their work, as

well as the necessity to think with its own head. **It's a real exhibition at the right time.**
Sonja Leboš

Your exhibition was an indication of what can be done with your life if you're persistent and have the guts to face all the obstacles. In doing so, you must have a solid vision that will guide you when, despite your undeniable talent, you doubt your strength. You had it all, and I congratulate you on that. I know there is not end with your activities because the restlessness in you won't let you. I wish you a lot of success in that.
 Marija Tuga Neral

Email to a friend

I believe you have received my short essay: The Dynamics of Everyday Life, where, among other things, at this time of isolation due to the Corona virus, I deal with my Great Monograph. It will show all the texts that have emerged in the last forty years: From my Memoirs, detailed descriptions of the design of the products and the presentation of the collected photographs from the presentation of my opus, the comparison of Croatian with the Canadian experience, "Thumbnails" from my life. Interviews for magazines and newspapers, well-intentioned comments, texts used at three exhibitions in Zagreb and Split will be included in the full, important speeches. In short, my life 'slalom' and a large number of historical facts about Croatian industrial design will be presented in the form of questions of the most knowledgeable people of cultural developments in Croatia and my answers.
In my design solutions I have always applied "less is more". I apply the same in my written materials – I have developed my own distinctive, fast-moving, rudimentary style, especially in "Collected Thumbnails from The Life of D. G." where I have forty stories. The book will have about 300 pages, including English translation.

Police station Brač

Hello,   April 1, 2020
I found you on the Internet so I'm checking in with you. I'm registered at this address in Supetar as well as my Nissan car. My wife and I went to visit our children in Toronto, Canada. That's where the CORONAVIRUS caught us. Canadian authorities recommend not travelling anywhere and especially NOT to Europe, where it is one of the Corona virus hotspots. We decided not to force a comeback until this situation calmed down (planes don't fly!) Registration and insurance expires in my Nissan By 20 May 2020, Obviously, I won't be able to extend it and do technical in time. I kindly ask that your station not send me a ticket for the delay in these exceptional circumstances! I'll get back to you and do it all as soon as I get to Supetar.
All right, take care.

Answer: In connection with your memo, we inform you that despite your vehicle being issued with a traffic license, you are not obliged to renew the same, all due to adverse circumstances caused by COVID, in accordance with the notice of the Ministry of Administrative Affairs.

Review of review

As you know I have invited some deserving colleagues to give me their contribution to my Great Monograph. There's no guarantee they'll do it. Throughout my life, I formed some of principles, so I remain only at one inquiry and possibly one reminder (it is human – to forget). It's a slightly different situation with you. Your entire analytical review will have on "weight". You are the only one who has an insight into all my creative activities and you can process them, put them in some context i.e. the impact on my creative work. Your education, art history and literature give you a wide range of considerations. I remember all those pleasures when working on: oil paintings, quick-moving sketches (Strumica, Brač, Vienna, Burgenland, Lovran, etc.), two-headed -awesome dragon, short stories depicted in "thumbnails". This could be called : "Diversity of creative engagements". My design opus was analyzed by Mark and Koraljka fairly. Some of their definitions surprised me, found me. From 1968 I have the title "First" and Mark gave me 50 years later: "The most productive Croatian industrial designer" I expect that you will not hesitate to suggest better - when "cleaning" all my texts. However, I will bring you my booklets with dedication!

My schoolmate Zvonko Kuharić (nephew of Cardinal Kuharić) wrote: "Your story should be published to our young people as a signpost in today's world of deranged values in which it is not popular to create and work, which is however the only true path to progress." With this publication his wish will be fulfilled! I'm especially pleased with that.

The list of good ones

Zvonimir Radić "Diša" (late) helped me a lot in my life's decision to leave everything in Zagreb and go to study industrial design in Vienna.

Goroslav Keller has followed me since my beginnings. His famous article: "Why did Davor Grünwald left? (1975.) perfectly describes the circumstances that made me leave. (Shown in Monograph). He proposed to ULUPUH's Lifetime Achievement Award 2017. for me.

Bernardo Bernardi (late) Senior colleague who wrote a beautiful accompanying text for the City of Zagreb Award. (Shown in Monograph)

Vladimir žitković (late) We spent together on several projects: Establishment of the Design Section (ULUPUH), Yu-Design, catamaran - from idea, to making molds and making parts for a catamaran. He was a great practitioner.

Anton Karavanić (late) We carried out several projects together: Establishment of the Design Section at ULUPUH, Implementation of Yu-Design from idea to realization.

Ana Lendvaj (late) Compiled a beautiful, informative newspaper article about my work, 1992. (Shown in Monograph)

Feđa Vukić Published an extensive newspaper article about my work in 1993. He later mentioned me in all his texts regarding industrial design. (Shown in Monograph)

Boris Ljubičić When B. Ljubičić says something everybody listens! He suggested to the MUO that my opus should be archived.

Koraljka Vlajo and Marko Golub performs as a duo. They started "processing" me in 2015. preparing an exhibition in HDD and later the exhibition in Split and this last one in TMNT. With their commemorative, intelligent texts, I was raised to the pedestal of Croatian industrial design. (Shown in Monograph)

Barbara Blasin A very talented graphic designer, her exhibition set-ups, graphic processing, is famous. I had a feeling that in my exhibitions and booklets she had given more than was expected of her.

Jaja Tomašković - Zane Dear high school classmate. She was present at all my achievements and always appropriately, intelligently commented.

Vlado and Zvonko Kuharić Colleagues from the eight-year school, always present at my important events with intelligent comments. (Shown in Monograph)

Jasna Lovrinčević Talented journalist who has recorded everything that has happened to me in recent years in her blog "In the Whirlwind of the Time". Six interviews! (Excerpts shown in Monograph)

Patricia Kiš Wrote a beautiful article in The Morning Newspaper: "Pioneer of design in the industry". (Shown in Monograph)

Željka Laslavić Published an extensive article in Lider magazine: "Davor Grünwald, pioneer of Croatian industrial design

Sanja Šegedin Miriovsky Extensive interview with me on HRT 1 in the show "Kultura"

Daniel Maxymiuk Canadian Ambassador opened my exhibition in HDD and on this occasion gave a landmark speech (Shown in Monograph)

Markita Franulić Director TMNT (Technical Museum, Nikola Tesla), the only one who responded to my 2014 memo, where I offer the theme of the exhibition with my accomplishments in 50 years. Other cultural institutions have never responded to me. Thanks to her belief that my opus is worth showing. this exhibition was realized at the end of 2019.

Prof. Boris Halasz Always ready to borrow TRS calculators from his collection

Peekpoke (Sveto) Always ready to borrow TRS calculators from his collection

Khristian Ilias (Sumate) Developed the supreme technological process when producing Sculptra

Rajka Maček Corrected my Croatian **Boris Ljubičić** When B. Ljubičić says something everybody listens! He suggested to the MUO that my opus should be archived.

Koraljka Vlajo and Marko Golub performs as a duo. They started "processing" me in 2015. preparing an exhibition in HDD and later the exhibition in Split and this last one in TMNT. With their commemorative, intelligent texts, I was raised to the pedestal of Croatian industrial design. (Shown in Monograph)

Barbara Blasin A very talented graphic designer, her exhibition set-ups, graphic processing, is famous. I had a feeling that in my exhibitions and booklets she had given more than was expected of her.

Jaja Tomašković - Zane Dear high school classmate. She was present at all my achievements and always appropriately, intelligently commented.

Vlado and Zvonko Kuharić Colleagues from the eight-year school, always present at my important events with intelligent comments. (Shown in Monograph)

Jasna Lovrinčević Talented journalist who has recorded everything that has happened to me in recent years in her blog "In the Whirlwind of the Time". Six interviews! (Excerpts shown in Monograph)

Patricia Kiš Wrote a beautiful article in The Morning Newspaper: "Pioneer of design in the industry". (Shown in Monograph)

Željka Laslavić Published an extensive article in Lider magazine: "Davor Grünwald, pioneer of Croatian industrial design

Sanja Šegedin Miriovsky Extensive interview with me on HRT 1 in the show "Kultura"

Daniel Maxymiuk Canadian Ambassador opened my exhibition in HDD and on this occasion gave a landmark speech (Shown in Monograph)

Markita Franulić Director TMNT (Technical Museum, Nikola Tesla), the only one who responded to my 2014 memo, where I offer the theme of the exhibition with my accomplishments in 50 years. Other cultural institutions have never responded to me. Thanks to her belief that my opus is worth showing, this exhibition was realized at the end of 2019.

Prof. Boris Halasz Always ready to borrow TRS calculators from his collection

Peekpoke (Sveto) Always ready to borrow TRS calculators from his collection

Khristian Ilias (Sumate) Developed the supreme technological process when producing Sculptra

Rajka Maček Corrected my Croatian text in Monograph

Ivo Hrvoić I worked for his company "Gem Systems" for 20 years as outside consultant.

Andrija Rusan Published large article about me in his architecture Magazine ORIS (Shown in Monograph)

Sonja Leboš Visited the exhibition in TMNT and self-initiated a wonderful article: "Industrial design tailored to man" in Vizkultura magazine. (Shown in Monograph)

Patricia Počanić I have a feeling, when the Corona virus and earthquake crisis passes in Zagreb, that she will accept the realization of my Monograph within ULUPUH.

List of bad ones

Mario Antonini - Director of the CIO (Center for Industrial Design). I was a "Thorn in his eye"! To keep me from working, he reported me to the police that I had an illegal studio. That didn't stop me. Through his communist channels, he imposed a ban on factories using the services of private persons. That's how he stabbed me "in the back". Professionally, he wasn't up to me, so he used that low means. The CIO, by its National function, was supposed to support me (and the others like me) and not compete with me. They received funding from the state: "To promote design", they should not have sought for jobs. The monopolistic aspirations of Antonini did not materialize. Yet the CIO (Antonini), with their communist ties, practically expelled me from Yugoslavia. However, since life has its legality, "thanks" to Antonini, I did not have to live in the immediate vicinity, of the horrors of the Home and War with Serbs.

Remarks: The Communists had their own interpretation of "Justice" based on greed.

My dad, Mladen, was blown up by mine, which was planted by communists, in 1944.
From my grandfather Josip was taken 80% of the estate. After that, he went mad and died.
My father-in-law Valko was picked up on the street and taken to The Naked Island (prison) without trial –he was neither guilty nor indebted.
What did they do to me? With their actions, restrictions, they expelled me from Yugoslavia.

Marijan Orešić We met in Vienna at the Academy. He studied sculpture and moved on to industrial design when he met me. We rented and shared room for a while. I was his best man at his wedding. I met him in Zagreb on the street when he finished his studies. I commented that I had been invited by the Director of the "Jadran" to take over the development of R&D. Marijan came to Jadran a few hours before my meeting and offered himself for the position! It's an incredible, almost criminal gesture! I don't understand how he could have survived as a professor in the Design Study with such a questionable character feature. I got that well-paid position. but had to leave after three months when I was conditioned to join the Communist Party.

Aleks Kuljiš Typical, narrow-minded, primitive, complex, jealous. Guys like that can give you a lot of headaches. I had to put up with him for 24 years at the Geonics.

The final word

While working on this monograph of mine, I recalled my life path, but now, looking back. I recalled all those nice moments, but also those awkward ones, luckily in smaller numbers.

From the context of this book, it is easy to discern the people who have supported me on my journey, to whom I am immensely grateful because without them it is difficult to know about me. Those who have restrained me with their misery and jealousy are also being mentioned. For them I have a message: your behavior has stimulated me for even better, even more intense activities! I never let those individuals interfere with my work.

I would be immensely pleased for this book to be in function as formulated by my classmate Zvonko Kuharić: "Your story should be published to our young people as a signpost in today's world of deranged values in which it is not popular to create and work, which is the only true path to progress."

Davors' sketches, 1964. – 1974.

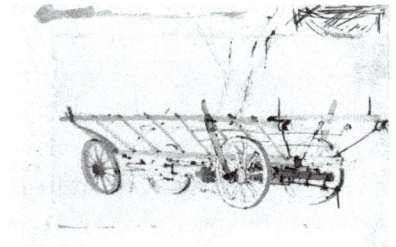

Redesign & design of mechanical, several electronic calculators, pocket calc. electr. scale, 1969-7

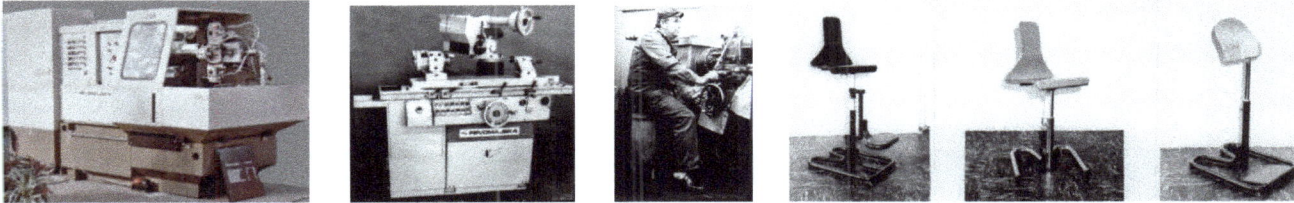

Redesign of machines tools for Prvomajska 1970.-1974. Industrial chairs for "Jadran", 1970.–1972.

Computer, tractor. folding stand, utensils. Genie, geophysical instr. Atomic absorption instr. 1075. – '85.

Fast ion printer: horizontal, vertical – office, Exhibition system 1980. – 1984.

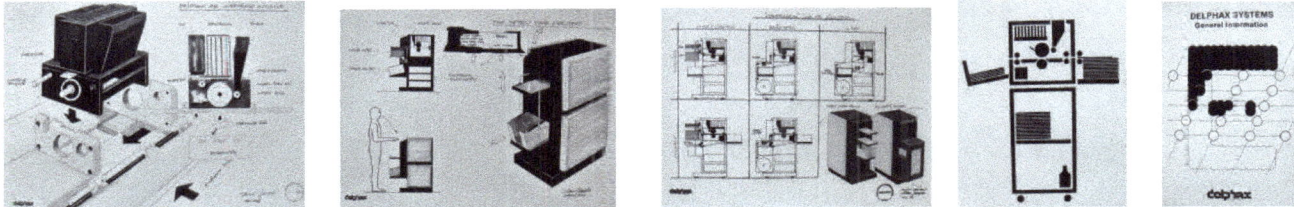

Sketches in connection with development of fast ion printers, 1980. – 1984.

Genie, antenna, winch, EM38 and EM61 geophysical instr. Radar geof. Instrument, 1984. – 1994..

Geophysical "bird"   Wine barbell   Elips chair   Control unit   Porsche Boxster rack

9 781649 690975